SACRAMENTO PUBLIC LIBRARY

3 3029 00332 0041

ART q745.51 H682 1976
1
Hobbs, Harr Veneer craft for ev
Schribner, c1976.
3 3029 00332 0041

D0459483

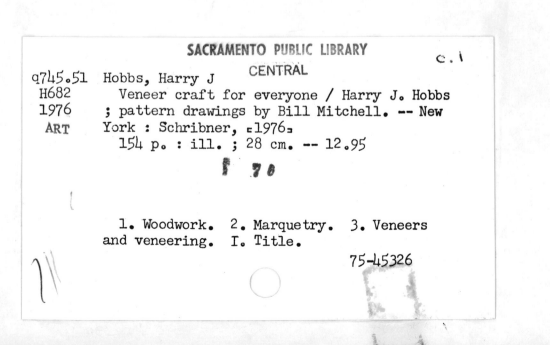

SACRAMENTO PUBLIC LIBRARY
CENTRAL   c. 1

q745.51   Hobbs, Harry J
H682   Veneer craft for everyone / Harry J. Hobbs
1976   ; pattern drawings by Bill Mitchell. -- New
ART   York : Schribner, c1976.
              154 p. : ill. ; 28 cm. -- 12.95

              1. Woodwork. 2. Marquetry. 3. Veneers
           and veneering. I. Title.
                                        75-45326

VENEER CRAFT FOR EVERYONE

VENEER CRAFT FOR EVERYONE

Harry J. Hobbs

PATTERN DRAWINGS BY

Bill Mitchell

CHARLES SCRIBNER'S SONS / NEW YORK

Copyright © 1976 Harry Jason Hobbs

Library of Congress Cataloging in Publication Data

Hobbs, Harry J
  Veneer craft for everyone.

  Includes index.
  1. Woodwork. 2. Marquetry. 3. Veneers and
veneering. I. Title.
TT200.H57   745.51   75-45326
ISBN 0-684-14614-2

THIS BOOK PUBLISHED SIMULTANEOUSLY IN
THE UNITED STATES OF AMERICA AND IN CANADA—
COPYRIGHT UNDER THE BERNE CONVENTION

ALL RIGHTS RESERVED. NO PART OF THIS BOOK
MAY BE REPRODUCED IN ANY FORM WITHOUT
THE PERMISSION OF CHARLES SCRIBNER'S SONS.

1 3 5 7 9 11 13 15 17 19 V/C 20 18 16 14 12 10 8 6 4 2

PRINTED IN THE UNITED STATES OF AMERICA

ACKNOWLEDGMENTS

To William Alexander Lincoln, Suffolk, England, and to Aleck H. Gordon, first president of the Marquetry Society of America, my lasting appreciation for getting me started by giving me personal instruction in knife-cutting marquetry techniques. To Mrs. Gertrude M. Constantine, president of Albert Constantine and Son, Inc., my special thanks for liberal supplies of choice veneers and equipment used in demonstration processes and projects. To my wife, Mary, my enduring gratitude for indispensable help with design ideas, photographic setups, and manuscript preparation. Thanks to Pat Bracewell for pattern drawings of "Undersea World," "Turtle Puzzle," "Chariot Horses," "Madonna," and "The Last Supper."

For technical research aid on veneers, my thanks to Donald H. Gott, executive director of Fine Hardwoods/American Walnut Association; to Forest Products Laboratory, U.S. Department of Agriculture; and to the New York Public Library, Technical Division. For technical research on early tools, I acknowledge with thanks two valuable sources: *The Carpenter's Tool Chest* by Thomas Hibben and *Ancient Carpenters' Tools* by Henry C. Mercer.

HARRY JASON HOBBS

CENTRAL
c. 1

CONTENTS

INTRODUCTION. Veneer Craft—Past, Present, and Future   *1*

1. How to Get Started   *4*

2. Veneers—Over One Hundred Kinds to Work With   *9*

3. Tools and Equipment   *13*

4. Designs and Patterns   *21*

5. Preparing Work Patterns   *25*

6. Selecting Veneers for Cutouts   *29*

7. Knife-Cutting Techniques   *34*

8. Saw-Cutting Techniques   *40*

9. Mounting Panels for Cutouts   *51*

10. Applying Cutouts   *59*

11. Filling Joints, Cleaning, Finishing   *65*

12. Advanced Veneering Techniques Simplified   *71*

13. Correcting Veneering Problems   *79*

14. Veneer Craft Projects   *83*

15. Introduction to Marquetry—Simplified Procedure   *147*

APPENDIX   *152*

INDEX   *153*

Veneer Craft— Past, Present, and Future

The art of inlaying colorful woods into contrasting wood surfaces to create artistic designs was practiced skillfully by the ancient Egyptians. From nearby copper mines they developed bronze, with which they made toothed blades to use as saws. Nature denied them an abundance of hardwood trees, so logs had to be imported, and their cost and scarcity presumably encouraged the enterprising Egyptians to get the most yardage from a log by sawing it into thin wood—the first veneers.

Precious examples of inlaid tables, jewel boxes, and panels 3,500 years old have come from Egyptian tombs, evidence that the Egyptians were the earliest recorded developers of both veneering and inlaying.

There are drawings and carvings, for instance, of saws and men working them against logs. There are pictures of men squatting before a low table, glue pot at one side, laying thin wood sheets onto a heavier surface, perhaps a tabletop.

The Romans borrowed from the Egyptians and went on to invent an ingenious bow saw that could cut veneers thinner than ever before. This discovery brought about advanced techniques of veneering and inlaying by the Roman artisans vying for high favor among the rulers and the rich.

The cultural artifacts of most civilizations since then indicate that wood was used increasingly in a purely decorative way. From furniture decoration the art developed into pictorial decoration in churches and palaces, and, at some later unrecorded time, inlay techniques were used to create individual wood pictures.

In the mid-sixteenth century, invention of the fret saw expanded pictorial inlay to pictorial marquetry. Separate parts of a picture were now saw-cut from veneers into segments of a design. These parts were fitted together, and the entire one-piece assembly was glued to a solid background. This procedure has a long history of names, but it is now generally called marquetry in America and England.

In very recent years, marquetry has been popular as a tabletop hobby. It is practiced both as a saw-cutting technique and a knife-cutting technique. Cutting small pieces of wood to fit intricately together is a skill that takes time and much patient practice to develop. It is a highly rewarding craft and it is the goal of many who want to try woodworking as a hobby. But marquetry is not easy for a beginner.

From many conversations with visitors at craft show demonstrations, it became clear to me that the majority of interested watchers want to try marquetry but shy away because it looks too difficult for a beginner, so I have developed veneer craft overlay. Its parentage is inlay and marquetry, but it is more attractive to beginners because it is so much easier.

With no forerunners for guidance, the techniques of overlay veneering demonstrated throughout this book have necessarily come from practical experience. Recorded marquetry techniques have been freely borrowed and altered to fit the special demands of veneer overlay, but hundreds of important little tricks practiced by skilled marquetarians and other artisans have never been recorded. So many of the procedures described here are of necessity the result of many experiments at the workbench.

Craft instructions do not separate easily into single-subject chapters. One aspect of a particular subject, glue coverage in Chapter 9, for example, relates to other information on gluing, such as cleanup of glue squeeze-out in Chapter 11 and veneer blisters, a direct result of poor gluing habits, in Chapter 13. Saw-cutting materials are introduced in Chapters 2 and 3 where emphasis is on *what*—what you need and what to use for particular types of work. Saw-cutting techniques are covered in Chapter 8 where emphasis is on *how*—how to saw-cut. This subject division is designed to make study easier and reference quicker. Once you have learned which saw blades to use (Chapter 3), you have learned all you need to know about saw blade selections, but you will often refer to saw-cut-

ting *how-to* in Chapter 8 for guidance in making a saw pad decision. The Table of Contents and the Index have been designed to be as effective as possible as guides for quick reference.

Some of the veneered projects you make will be purely decorative—pictures on a wall—and some things will be utilitarian—boxes, coasters, serving trays, planters. But there is still another opportunity in veneer craft. The activity you start as a hobby could grow into a profitable spare-time occupation.

Veneered boxes, for example, sell reasonably well through gift shops, although your profit is likely to be only moderate. First, suppose you pay about $4 for an unfinished craft box. You veneer it at a cost of 50¢ for veneer and 20¢ for replacement hinges. You sell it to the gift shop for $8 on consignment; that is, you get paid after the shop sells the box for $12. You might try it out by taking finished boxes to your local gift shop. You won't get rich veneering boxes, but you will have a rewarding hobby which also brings in a little money.

The materials for small picture plaques, however, cost much less than materials for boxes. The total cost for "Wild Horses" (page 114), veneer and hardboard panel, is no more than $1, and a horse fancier might pay up to $50 for this plaque. Pretty good wages!

Larger pictures bring higher prices, yet the materials cost is still only a few dollars. Large panoramic displays are very popular. There are three notable examples in this book: "Africa," "Prehistoric America," and "Undersea World." Time and again, people who have seen these panels have said, "Let me know if you decide to sell!"

If these prospects aren't encouragement enough for planning a walk to the bank, consider these actual sales by a marquetry

Figure 1. Picture gallery. Standardizing the size of mounting panels is a work convenience and a display advantage. Vertical subjects can then fit into one gallery arrangement as illustrated, and horizontal subjects, on the same size panel turned on edge, fit into a second gallery. Strips of rabbeted molding attached to the wall provide tracks for sliding panels into position. Titles of these plaques: "White Roses," "Mexico," "Birds in Flight," and "First Swimming Lesson."

picture craftsman in California. His panels measured from 16″ x 24″ to 20″ x 33″. A "Matterhorn" picture sold for $650. An "American Eagle," $650. One "Cypress of Monterey" panel brought $1,200, another "Cypress," slightly larger, brought $1,500. This craftsman is now a professional, but he started as a hobbyist.

How do you start selling your pictures?

One way is to set up your own gallery show at home after you have completed twenty or thirty good pictures. Ask the Home Page editor of your local newspaper to announce your art show. Offer photographs of a few panels to run with the news story, or invite the staff photographer to take his own. Your ingenuity will find a way to bring people to a new type of gallery show.

CHAPTER 1

How to Get Started

Veneer craft is a simplified form of woodworking used for decorative purposes.

Veneer is thin wood, sliced from the world's finest hardwood logs by huge 17-foot slicing knives. Veneer is the only material involved in the designs in this book. It is a surprisingly strong and stable material, uniquely figured and richly colored by nature.

Craft is the system of working techniques developed to cut, sand, assemble, and glue veneer parts into designs and surface treatments.

Veneer craft could be called overlay marquetry. Overlay means applying separate cutout parts of a design onto a mounting panel instead of cutting all parts, including the background, to fit intricately into one level surface as in true marquetry. Overlay is an easier process. For example, the large panoramic scene of Africa on page 120 uses the overlay method. Only an experienced marquetarian could make this panel as a marquetry picture, but any beginner in veneer craft with a few months of practice could make and assemble a praiseworthy "Africa Panorama."

What you make by cutting veneers to follow the shape of a design can become a wood picture to be used as a wall hanging. You can make an easel-backed memento plaque for desk or chest, an applied decoration for any wood surface, a brain-twister puzzle, a mobile, a woman's purse box, a jewel box, or personalized costume jewelry.

For a beginning, it would be wise to choose a subject that offers the most practice using the smallest amount of veneer. Start with the small parts that compose "Sports Figures" (page 83), for example. Without wasting a lot of wood, you can make, and remake if necessary, one small piece at a time. This design can teach you the important fundamentals of knife-cutting, the first step in veneer craft.

After your sports training lessons, you will be able to cut most one-piece designs without wasting valuable veneer. Many of the African animals are simple one-piece designs requiring no fitted parts. "Flying Angel" is just as easy (Figure 2), and "Birds in Flight" is not at all difficult if you follow the knife-cutting procedures outlined in Chapter 7, especially the methods for cutting sharp points like bird beaks and wing tips. You will be ready for these projects after you have invested a few hours in practice cutting the curved pieces in "Sports Figures."

Figure 2. One-piece design of angel represents the easiest type of cutout to make. Trace full-size pattern to avodire and cut outline with craft knife. Mount on panel veneered with purpleheart.

Next you may be ready for the two-piece "Bighorn I" (Figure 3) or your choice from a wide collection of designs provided in Chapter 14.

To begin, you need a sufficient number of small sheets of veneer which provide contrast in color and figure. Figure is the correct term for what is often called grain. Veneer is sold in sheets measuring from 4″ x 9″ to approximately 12″ x 36″ and in two thicknesses, ¹/₂₈″ and ¹/₄₀″. To distinguish between the two thicknesses you will work with, count seven sheets of this book. Except that veneer is stiffer than paper, you are feeling the approximate thickness of ¹/₂₈″ veneer. Hold four sheets and you are feeling the approximate thickness of ¹/₄₀″ veneer.

Tools are your next requirement. Actually you can get started with items you probably already own, plus one new tool—a craft knife.

Figure 3. "Bighorn I" is a two-piece cutout which involves simply joining the two parts, walnut animal and zebrano rock. Mounting panel was veneered with myrtle, swirl figure (full-size pattern, Chapter 5).

BASIC WORKSHOP. A typical assortment (Figure 4) of essential items for making cutouts by the knife-cutting method includes:

sharpening stone
12″ rule
straightedge made by filing teeth off discarded hacksaw blade
single-edge razor blade
craft knife in cork protector
sandpaper wrapped around a block of wood

emery board
parts workbox
clear adhesive tape
sharp pencil
black carbon paper
roll of wax paper
squeeze-bottle white glue
tweezers
glue brush with tip pruned
tin can
old brick
workboard, a lumberyard cutoff of flakeboard

How much will it cost to get started with a veneer craft workshop for the knife-cutting method? One box of assorted 4″ x 9″ veneers and one craft knife will cost about six or seven dollars, depending upon local prices. If you lack some of the other items on the basic workshop list, you probably still can get everything you need for less than ten dollars.

WORKSHOP NUMBER 2. For the saw-cutting method, you must add a few items to your basic workshop. Figure 5 shows an assortment of these items:

1-foot steel square
spiral hand drill
fret saw with blades

Figure 4. Basic workshop consists of items rounded up at home, plus the most important tool in the veneer craft workshop, the craft knife. (Notice knife point stuck in cork for safety.)

homemade bird's-mouth saw table
C-clamp to secure saw table

In the section on tools and equipment, Chapter 3, you will find additional items that will make your work easier and more professional.

Space requirements for a basic workshop are very modest. A sturdy worktable is all you need, except for a chest drawer or a shelf to store materials. Workshop Number 2 can be set up within the same modest space, but this shop produces sawdust—not much, but enough to bar you from the dining room table and carpeted areas.

From the variety of designs in Chapter 14 you will surely find a few of your favorite subjects. In addition to the photographs

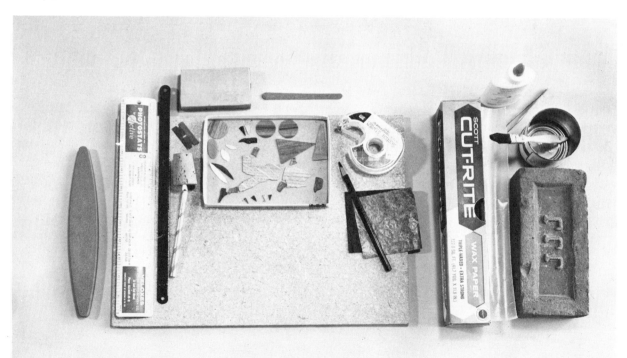

Figure 5. Workshop Number 2 supplements the basic shop with items needed for saw-cutting veneer designs.

of finished models to show you what your veneer craft cutouts will look like, there are dozens of line drawings of the designs. These line drawings are your full-size patterns, ready to be traced and transferred to cutting materials.

In the beginning, it is always advisable to follow prepared patterns drawn by professional artists who are familiar with the characteristics of thin veneer. After you have had working experience with veneers and the special techniques of pattern breakup, you can start creating your own designs.

CHAPTER 2

Veneers—Over One Hundred Kinds to Work With

Veneers are hardwoods, best suited to veneer craft because they are strong, close-grained, hard-surfaced woods. They are the glamorous woods of the world in color and figure. It took one hundred to one hundred and twenty years for the average hardwood tree to grow large enough for harvest, and some are in dwindling supply. Most veneers come from trees cut in deep jungles where vegetation is lush. In some countries, elephants are still taught to drag the gigantic logs to truck depots for transport to rivers or seacoasts where ships pick them up and bring them to America for cutting into fine lumber and veneer. More than a hundred veneers are available, and they vary greatly in color and figure pattern. A few of the descriptive names you will come to recognize are purpleheart, satinwood, African cherry, lacewood, zebrawood, ebony, East Indian rosewood, and tulipwood.

Veneers are not available at your local lumberyard, but you can usually purchase or order them from a woodworkers' supply house. Some shops have a mail-order service.

Since you don't yet know veneers by name, your best course in the beginning is to buy a box of forty assorted kinds, size 4″ x 9″ (Figure 6). This variety provides you with plenty of material for a large number of cutouts. Many of the cutouts in Chapter 14 can be made with these sheets, as the parts of the designs are seldom larger than about 6″. This size isn't very useful for backgrounds, although you could select and arrange three sheets for a sky, mountain, and field background. The assortment package identifies each veneer by name. For future projects and for making backgrounds for mounting panels, you can order specific veneers by name and in larger sheets. Meanwhile, you can examine the figure patterns of quite a few popular veneers in the photographs of projects and working procedures throughout this book.

Aside from the small sheets, veneers are customarily sold in 3-foot lengths. Widths vary with the kind of wood. Mahogany, oak, butternut, African cherry, walnut, primavera, avodire, sycamore, and others are generally available in 12″ widths. Some varieties from small-trunked trees and noted as such in woodworkers' catalogs, are only 5″ or slightly more in width. When

Figure 6. Introductory assortment of veneers offered by wood suppliers provides a wide variety of color and figure pattern for making many of the designs in this book.

you are ready to select 3-foot lengths, the following list should be helpful.

Avodire and Primavera. Quite similar in color, from off-white to pale gold. Good for light skies, lakes, and fields and where cutouts are dark and require a pale background for contrast. Avodire is likely to have a more interesting figure than primavera. Example of avodire sky: "Bighorn II" in Chapter 15. Example of primavera: sky in "Mexico."

Bird's-eye Maple. The dyed white variety,

$1/40''$ thick, makes excellent background for contrasting subjects. Interesting burl-type figure.

Butternut. Figure resembles the arrowheads in oak. Color is between oak and light walnut. Easier to knife-cut than either oak or walnut. A handsome, useful wood, important in the starter kit.

Chinawood. Is $1/40''$ thick. Tan with an overall yellowish tinge, flecked and streaked with purplish red figure. Resembles tulipwood. Resembles bubinga in color, but has much straighter figuration than bubinga. Chinawood looks like the western sky at sunset, and when cut diagonally it makes a rocky precipice as in "Bighorn II" marquetry picture.

Gulf-Stream Green. A chemically treated wood in a soft shade of green. Minimal figure, but some has just enough wavy figure to depict ocean, lake, or carpeted floor of the forest. Example: foreground in "Prehistoric America."

Gumwood. Irregular, prominent figure. Exhibits a mixture of shades ranging from dark brown to light brown and tan. Excellent for mountains, coastlines, rain clouds in the sky. Generally comes about 6″ wide. See examples of gumwood mountains in Chapter 14: "Mexico," "Africa," and "Prehistoric America."

Mahogany. Plain and stripe veneers vary from light reddish brown tones to deep shades. Stripe figure is straight, but quite faint in some sheets. Useful where figure should not contribute to the subject. Should be in every starter assortment.

Oak, U.S.A. White oak preferred. Arrowhead figure with straight or diagonal stripes useful as sky, water, fields, birds, paths, and roads. Straw color. Example: background for "Midnight Ride of Paul Revere."

Sycamore. Light tan, some with a faint pink tint. Mild, wavy grain, sometimes very faint. Excellent as a light-colored background. Examples: sky in "Prehistoric America"; complete background for "Wild Horses."

Walnut. Plain or stripe. Useful as an entire background if cutouts are predominantly lighter or darker than walnut. Butt walnut makes good trees, as in "Africa" and "Lion's Pride."

Zebrano and Tamo Ash. Choose only one for a starter kit. Both are tan, with a prominent brown figure. Zebrano has straight or slightly wavy stripes. Leaf-figured tamo is much wilder generally, but some has small, fine, wavy figure. Tamo makes the best ocean waves, from calm to stormy. Neither of these two veneers should be used in more than one-fourth of a background panel.

Veneers vary in thickness. Until the last few years, $1/28″$ was the standard American thickness. The worldwide trend now is toward thinner veneers, generally $1/40″$. The 4″ x 9″ assortment consists mostly of $1/28″$ veneers. They require a little more time and patience to knife-cut than to saw-cut. American supply houses now offer assorted packs of $1/40″$ veneers also, usually from six to ten kinds. This is less of a selection than the 4″ x 9″ assortment, but is a good purchase. One of the $1/40″$ packs supplied all veneer used for "Sports Figures."

Consider veneer thickness when you buy veneers. Unfortunately, even a supplier cannot be certain that veneer standards will remain constant from one shipment to the next. Occasionally you will find yourself working with two thicknesses, $1/28″$ and $1/40″$, but this difference is seldom critical. Marquetarians are accustomed to working with a mixture. If two thicknesses adjoin in a marquetry picture, the thicker edge is feathered with sandpaper or the entire picture is sanded down to one level. You can do the same.

Dyed veneers: Most veneers you work with are natural woods. Only two, one pink and one green, out of forty in the 4″ x 9″ assortment are chemically dyed woods. A few craftsmen object to the use of dyed woods, but many other crafts rely largely on dyed materials. Potters add chemical oxide dyes to clay, artists work with dyed colors, those who knit, embroider, or weave use dyed wool. It would seem that dyed woods should be welcomed by those who do pictorial veneering. Before you form your own opinion about dyed woods, you may want to see what an important part they play in some of the designs in this book.

Dyed woods can add lively accent to veneer pictures. You can draw on a rainbow of colors, some bright, others pastel. The newest variety is beautiful bird's-eye maple dyed white. The dyeing process apparently makes wood more brittle; remember to cut dyed woods with extra caution.

Veneer edging: Thin, flexible veneer for edging panels comes in two widths, 1″ and 2″, in 8-foot rolls. The 1″ size is easier to handle. It is available in six different woods: mahogany, walnut, teak, oak, birch, and Korina, which is nearest to white. This real wood edging, called wood trim, adds a finished appearance to your panels. Do not substitute imitation wood trim made of plastic. It detracts from your veneer cutout.

Assembled veneer faces: When you are ready to try a few veneering projects, such as covering ready-made unfinished small boxes with figured veneer, you may wish to add decorative designs to the box lids. One of the quickest ways to do this is to buy ready-made veneer faces and either inlay them in the lid or overlay them. An extensive variety of ready-to-use faces is available. They come assembled with gummed tape on one side, removable with water after the gluing is done. See Chapter 12 for full instructions.

CHAPTER 3

Tools and Equipment

KNIVES. The knife to use for cutting veneers is the pencil type with a knurled sleeve which tightens the chuck (often called an X-acto knife). This feature permits a quick change of blade.

For working convenience keep several knives bladed and ready for use. Mark your set of knives with different colors so you can distinguish the sharpest blade from the one you use for noncritical cutting or utility jobs such as cutting tape. To paint a knife handle, spiral a piece of masking tape around the entire length of the handle and spray on a colored enamel or color with a felt tip marker. The pot full of knives is a working convenience, not a necessity. An empty glass jar, packed with a chunk of Styrofoam to protect knife points, makes an excellent holder, safe for the worker and easy to reach (Figure 7). The knob-handled knife in the center of this knife pot is solely for utility.

KNIFE BLADES. The No. 11 X-acto blade is best for cutting veneer. It is thin, sharply pointed, and tapered. It is sold at hobby counters everywhere, as is the knife. Don't consider your pocketknife a suitable substitute. It is too thick for cutting a close-fitting joint.

Only one other style of blade was used for the projects in this book, a chisel blade that fits the same kind of knife. It is useful for trimming narrow bits of veneer which you sometimes will need to replace a broken tip. It is also used constantly for cleanup work.

SHARPENING STONE. Any fine-grain stone is satisfactory. The best type for knives is a small, hard Arkansas stone. Don't use an oilstone you may have on hand. Oil residue will stain veneer, and the used stone probably is no longer flat. Frequent whetting on the stone restores sharpness to the point where you need it, but a fresh blade usually is better for critical cutting.

WORKBOARD/CAUL BOARD. You need a semisoft, smooth workboard to lay veneers on when you cut with knife or veneer saw. The preferred workboard is known as flakeboard or particle board. It is available at lumberyards where it can be bought in random-sized cutoffs, or for a few cents more you can have it cut to your requirements. Buy ⅜″ or ½″ thickness and get several sizes for various projects. Handy ap-

13

Figure 7. Glass jar packed with tight chunk of Styrofoam makes a safe, visible keeper for craft knives. Pointed blade at left is best for cutting veneer.

ferent areas and use both sides. Small panels of hardboard also make good workboards for knife-cutting veneer parts. After a workboard has been scratched up considerably, it is less useful for cutting veneer. However, it now makes a better mounting panel for cutouts, as the scratches improve the bonding power of glue.

STRAIGHTEDGE. The straightedge most often photographed in this book, and the handiest, is a discarded hacksaw blade with its teeth ground down so that they cannot scratch hands or wood.

A steel square serves a double function: straightedge and layout tool. You can get by with a 12″ metal square; in fact, you will have to improvise to get by without it. When getting out squares of veneer, you need a layout tool that gives you a true right-angle corner. The steel square is the handiest tool for such layouts.

GLUES. If you buy only one type of glue to begin with, buy white squeeze-bottle glue, such as Elmer's (Figure 8). It is the most important kind for veneer craft. It sets quickly, but not too quickly for last-second adjustment of a cutout part. It holds well and is colorless when dry. It is the easiest glue to clean up after it has dried.

A second kind, Titebond, is also a squeeze-bottle glue. It sets faster, holds curled veneers better, but is somewhat stiffer to spread and a little harder to clean up when dry. Both kinds are easily removed from hands and brushes with water.

An instant-contact adhesive, like Veneer Glue brand, is essential for gluing veneer edging to mounting panels and is preferred for surfaces larger than about one square foot.

proximate sizes are 9″ x 12″, 10″ x 13″, 11″ x 15″, and 12″ x 16″.

You should buy boards in pairs whenever possible, since you will borrow from your assortment of workboards when you need caul boards to clamp a panel you are gluing. You need two cauls for every gluing job and they should be approximately the same size or they will be hard to clamp.

Veneer saw and knife will cut through veneer and scratch your workboard. To distribute the wear, do your cutting in dif-

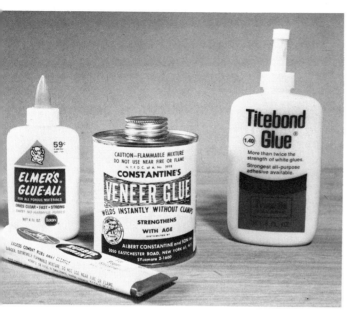

Figure 8. White squeeze-bottle glue is the basic one to use (far left). For some types of work, the other two will do better. Rubber cement is used only for patterns.

Rubber cement is useful for sticking paper patterns to saw pads, but using it directly on veneer is risky because it may stain the wood. Vinegar, although not a perfect remedy, removes most of the stain.

GLUING AIDS. The accessories which are most helpful when gluing cutout parts to mounting panels and laying face and back veneers on panels are shown in Figure 9. A ½″ brush is the handiest size for small work. Provide a glass jar or a can to hold the brush, since you will frequently need both hands while you are gluing. Drop the brush, handle first, in the jar keeper.

For spreading glue quickly over large areas, make a glue spreader. Cut notches in one edge of a scrap piece of ⅛″ or ¼″ wood. Leave the points square or they will break off easily. Nothing fancier than the spreader shown is needed (or will work any better).

Two rollers are shown. The small wooden roller is most useful for applying hard pressure on freshly glued assemblies. Awl, or pin for tiny parts, prevents veneer or panel from sliding while you spread glue. Tweezers help you move glue-fresh parts to a mounting surface.

WEIGHTS. When you are gluing cutout parts or sheets of veneer to a mounting panel, you need weights. Heavy antique flatirons and sections of rail are ideal; they weigh the most for their size. Bricks are next best and easier to find. Chip off old mortar to make a smooth brick. Get plenty of bricks; I keep nine on hand. Wrap at least one brick in a paper or plastic bag, and keep it within reach. It makes a clean hold-down for work in progress and a temporary weight for small glued parts until you are ready to lay a caul over the work and put several bricks on top.

Figure 9. Gluing aids are for spreading, assembling cutout parts, and rollering veneer for good contact. Homemade wooden comb is a spreader.

Figure 10. The C-clamp (left) is essential—the others are welcome aids. Always buy clamps in pairs so you can apply equal pressure, one clamp across from its mate.

CLAMPS. You can make every project in this book without clamps if you have two heavy iron weights and about four bricks, or no iron and eight bricks to pile one on top of another. It is safer, however, to clamp glued work that measures over a foot square or work that involves veneer that is slightly buckled. Veneer that is badly buckled must first be flattened (see Chapter 15).

The first clamps to buy are C-clamps with a 3″ jaw opening (Figure 10). You will never need more jaw opening but can use to good advantage the deeper throat of the 4″ size. They usually cost twice as much, however. A good assortment would be two of each size; otherwise four small clamps will do.

After C-clamps, spring clamps are the most useful. They are like extra hands. Get two clamps with a 2″ jaw opening, a large size for this type of clamp.

The wood-jaw handscrew is the cabinet-maker's right hand. If you buy any for craftwork, get one with a 4½″ opening. The long jaw reaches closer than C-clamps to the center of most veneer craft glue jobs. Buy clamps in even numbers so that the same pressure can be applied at opposite edges of the panel being glued.

CAULS. This term is widely used in veneering but is not generally known among beginners. Cauls are wood or flakeboard forms which conform to the shape of other work. In this book we are concerned only with flat cauls, preferably flakeboard panels, to be placed on top of and under a glued panel or a glued cutout assembly laid on a mounting panel to dry. Two cauls are required for every glue-up, regardless of how you are applying pressure while the glue dries.

For panel veneering, clamps are preferred to weights. The cauls you use for a clamping setup are discussed in Chapter 9. Cauls needed for glue-ups being weighted are explained in Chapter 10. Fir plywood should not be used as a caul for pressing against veneer. Under heavy pressure it

Figure 11. Veneer saw is a better tool than craft knife for making straight cuts when getting a work sheet out of larger veneer sheet. Some saws, such as this one, come with the coarser teeth in the cutting position. Before cutting veneer, remove two screws and reverse blade to put fine teeth in the natural cutting position.

imprints the veneer. This is known in the trade as "telegraphing."

VENEER SAW. This small, double-edged hand saw is the best tool for making straight cuts in veneer (Figure 11). Its only function is to get out work-size sheets of veneer (from which you will then cut parts), and it does this better than a knife, which can be pulled away from the straightedge by stubborn grain. The veneer saw is especially good for cutting sheets of veneer to a required size for a saw pad.

FRET SAWS. The style illustrated in the basic workshop is the handiest, most practical style you can buy for small work. It has an 8″ throat and an adjustable frame to accommodate blades from 6″ down to 3¼″ broken segments. Best of all, it is the easi-

est style to handle when you are inserting (called threading) a blade through a new starting hole in a saw pad. You will come to appreciate this convenience.

The second style of fret saw you might want is the large model shown here (Figure

Figure 12. Fret saw with deep throat can saw to the center of large saw pads, where a smaller fret saw cannot reach.

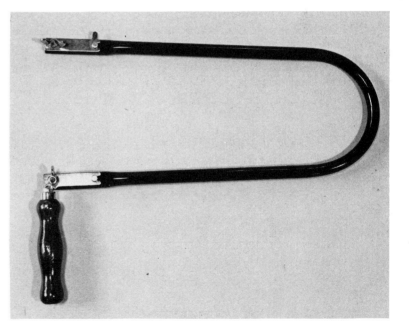

12). It costs only about one-third as much as the smaller fret saw, and it has a 12″ throat. This larger style is necessary for larger work. Its blade can reach the center of a 23″ circle. This tool will not grip a blade of less than 5″, meaning that broken blades cannot be used. At first, you will find it a bit awkward to thread. Refer to Chapter 8 for some suggested handling habits.

SAW BLADES. Only plain-end blades are used in fret saws. Pin-end blades for coping saws are much too coarse for cutting thin veneers. Coping saws have no place in veneer craft. Start with three grades of fret-saw blades: 6J6 is a sturdy blade. It is 6″ long and has 32 teeth to the inch, the coarsest you can use. Type 4J is fine, 5″ long, with 40 teeth to the inch. Type 3/0 is 5″ long, 66 teeth to the inch, very fine, very brittle. Use it only on close-fitting work and then only on thin saw pads. Type 3/0 blade breaks at the slightest quick twist of the saw frame.

Figure 13. During fret-sawing, saw pads are supported on a bird's-mouth which is clamped on the edge of the worktable as an extension.

Fret saws are used for sawing veneer to required shapes. Sawing is done only when the veneer is held between heavier sheets of wood. One or more sheets of veneer may be layered, that is, laid one on another, to make what is known as a saw pad or a sandwich.

WOOD FOR SAW PADS. For the saw-cutting method, you need wood to make protective saw pads. Three kinds of wood fill all saw pad requirements. Balsa alone will fill most requirements.

Balsa in recommended thickness of $3/32″$ comes 2″, 3″, 4″, and 6″ wide. You save money buying the 6″ width and cutting it down when necessary, but much of the time you need the 6″ width. Pads larger than 6″ can be made by joining pieces with gummed paper tape. Don't use clear tape. A useful substitute, and a handy wood to have on hand, is $1/28″$ poplar. It is thinner than balsa and available in wider sheets.

A second grade of poplar is stronger and harder than balsa. Buy $1/8″$ thickness for large pads that cannot be nailed because of the design. You cannot cut anything heavier. In this thickness, it comes 8″ wide (sometimes up to 12″) in lengths of 36″.

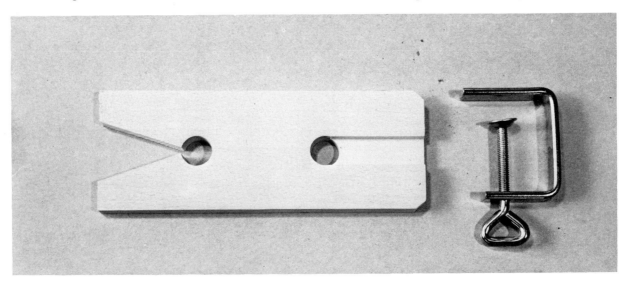

SAW TABLE AND CLAMP. When you cut veneer with a fret saw, the veneer is layered in a saw pad. The pad must be supported on a table called a bird's-mouth. The unit shown here measures only 7″ long and is recessed for its own clamp (Figure 13). It attaches to the worktable.

A larger, homemade saw table is shown in the photograph of the Number 2 workshop. It was made of ¾″ x 7″x 15″ scrap pine. In one end a V-notch was cut 2½″ deep, ending in a small hole at the throat. The hole will grow as your saw nicks into it. Eventually you need a new bird's-mouth. Cut a notch in the opposite end of the board.

DRILL. Fret-saw blades require starting holes through the saw pad. The best-size drill bit to use is ⁵/₆₄″. You may already own a crank-style hand drill, push drill, electric drill, or a banana-size motorized hand grinder. They all have chucks that can hold a ⁵/₆₄″ bit.

WORKBOXES. Provide your worktable with two flat cardboard boxes to protect working veneer from breakage. Use one as a materials box, holding sheets of veneer ready for a saw pad or ready to be knife-cut. Drop leftovers in here too. Use the second box for cut-out veneer parts waiting for assembly on a panel.

TOOL BOX. Store your small tools in a shallow box. Store loose, used blades in clear plastic pill containers in the box together with scissors, rule, gummed tape—all the miscellany. It may look disorganized, but a tool box is a great time-saver.

MISCELLANY. Three kinds of tape are useful: ⅜″ clear, ½″ masking, and 1″ light-weight gummed paper tape sold by stationers and woodworking suppliers. A small stiff-bristled brush removes sanding dust from the pores of veneer and cleans your workboard of damaging sawdust, sanding grit, and shards of veneer. Half-inch brads, driven into waste areas, stabilize a floppy saw pad.

SANDPAPER AND ACCESSORIES. Garnet paper, identified by its reddish color, is fast-cutting and usually preferred for raw wood. Two grades will fill your needs: 150-C and 180-A. The higher the number, the finer the grit. A third grade called finishing paper, tan colored, grade 220 or 240, belongs in your supply box for the finest work. The finer grades are the ones to use when preparing sanding sticks (Figure 14).

Make a small variety of sanding sticks. In addition to the essential hand-size block of wood or cork wrapped with sandpaper, several shapes of sanding sticks are needed. Wrap finishing paper around an assortment of round dowels, half-round molding scraps, and square sticks. Cut 4½″ lengths of ⅛″ and ¼″ dowels and a piece of broomstick, and cut one or two strips of thin, flat scrap such as balsa. Apply sandpaper to sticks by coating sandpaper and stick with rubber cement. Supplement the highly useful collection of sanding sticks with a few cosmetic counter emery boards.

POWER JIG SAWS. This modern, mechanized fret saw is sometimes called a power scroll saw. Do not confuse it with the power hand sabre saw which in recent years has often been called a jig saw. You won't need a sabre saw in veneer craft. Two types of jig saw are useful. The less expensive is a magnetic oscillating type with a self-contained power unit. Its trade

Figure 14. Sanding sticks for perfecting sawed or knife-cut edges of cutouts should be made in a variety of shapes.

name is Dremel. It requires a short pin-end blade. Two blades are available, but only the finer blade is suitable, and it can be used only for cutting sandwiched saw pads. It leaves a wide kerf that is objectionable where close-fitting and interlocking parts are involved; yet it is fast and completely satisfactory for cutting bold, sweeping outlines.

The best model for veneer craft is the Rockwell scroll saw, which costs a bit more than one hundred dollars. It has a separate motor and operates at several speeds. Its special chucks take plain-end blades, which means that you can use blades so fine you have to feel for the direction of the teeth.

These finer blades do not break as frequently in a jig saw as you might imagine, because the work swivels around on a flat table and does not jiggle up and down as it has a tendency to do on a fret-saw table. Marquetarians like this machine for its fine, fast action.

Power jig saws are an asset in any veneer craft workshop, but they can ruin your work in a hurry unless you constantly remember to feed the work more slowly than the machine can rip through it. At a very slow work-feed you can do highly accurate cutting. You guide the work with two hands, an advantage over one-hand guiding in hand fret-saw work.

CHAPTER 4

Designs and Patterns

Design ideas for veneer craft come from nature, history, the Bible, sports, mythology, legends, folk art, and many other pictorial sources. An adaptable object, theme, or scene must be something that can be expressed in outline. This is a basic requirement of working with veneer. In other words, the pattern you make cannot depict a trailing line of wispy cloud or ocean wave. The cloud or wave must be a connected outline of sufficient size to be cut from veneer. The piece must be stable enough to be handled without splintering. The most suitable subjects, therefore, are those that can be attractively expressed without a lot of detail. Admittedly, professionals have little tricks for making very thin lines appear as trailing clouds, feathery bird tails, and similar effects, but the beginner should not attempt them.

To convert your own design ideas into work patterns, start by tracing a design you have located. Next, make a second tracing of your first, drawing only the outline. Add details sparingly. Remember, you will be cutting out everything you draw. Include only those details that you can cut as complete pieces of veneer and assemble either by joining them to the main outline or gluing them on top of it. Every detail is to become a single piece of veneer.

As a practice example of veneer craft design principles, study the Tree of Life, now a popular theme in pottery, weaving, embroidery, and painting. From the drawing of "Tree of Life" (Figure 15) you can learn a lot about veneer designing. It seems too obvious to point out, but veneer is a three-dimensional medium. Painting is two-dimensional.

In "Tree of Life," all leaves, branches, and birds are separate pieces. Following this design technique, create your own "Tree of Life." Avoid intricate joints and keep components separated wherever possible. Make a full-size work pattern. Trace the pieces of your design on chosen veneers, and go to work with your craft knife.

If you are not an accomplished artist, you could hardly pick a better theme as an exercise in designing. The shapes require a minimum of drawing ability. As an exercise in knife-cutting it also has much to offer. First of all, there is a lot to practice on; and second, its free-form shapes place no exacting demands on your knife-cutting skill. Outline irregularities in the parts are

Figure 15. Drawing of "Tree of Life" pattern serves as model from which to learn principles of designing for veneer cutouts. If you like to learn by doing, now make your own "Tree of Life" pattern and knife-cut the parts from veneer.

fairly correctable by light sanding, and any remaining mistakes will not be conspicuous in a busy design. When you have completed "Tree of Life," you are ready for more advanced designs.

In Chapter 14 you will find many ready-to-trace patterns, ranging from simple to advanced. To transfer these patterns to veneer or saw pad, either trace them onto tracing paper or make photocopies of the page. (Photocopies are much more accurate than tracings.)

Large woodworkers' supply houses usually offer a wide range of work-size patterns drawn especially for veneer craftsmen. Subjects include flying ducks, midnight owls, flowers, Christmas ornaments, pussycats, tigers, Noah's arks, cypresses of Monterey, wild sweetbriar roses, American folk designs, and many other popular subjects.

For knife-cutting, you need a pattern from which you can trace one part at a time, saving the pattern for possible reuse. For saw-cutting, the pattern is expendable. In fact, you usually need two identical patterns. With scissors, cut apart the various components of the design. Cement one part at a time to the saw pad and cut it along with the wood.

HOW TO ENLARGE OR REDUCE DESIGNS.
When a design is too small or too large for your project, one way to change the size is to have a photostat copy made. For about a dollar and a half, you can enlarge a copy to twice its original size or reduce it by half—or any size in between. Then either trace the photostat and use the tracing as your work pattern or have a few photocopies made of the photostat.

A drawing instrument called a pantograph, consisting of four pivoting wood or metal strips, provides another way of enlarging or reducing designs. Without either of these facilities, resort to the dependable graph-square method.

You can buy printed graph-square sheets from art supply stores and large stationers. To enlarge a design, use a colored pencil to draw small graph squares on the original design. If you don't want to mark up the original, place it under tracing paper, fix its position with tape, and draw squares on the tracing paper.

If you have drawn ⅛" squares on the original and want a pattern twice as large as the original, for example, do your plotting on the printed graph-square sheet using ¼" squares. To make a reduced pattern, use larger original squares and smaller pattern sheet squares. The printed graph-square sheets save time and assure accuracy, but of course you can draw up your own graph sheets if you prefer.

There is also an easier way to enlarge and reduce on graph squares. It is illustrated here. It makes use of a reusable printed grid sheet of celluloid. Squares are ⅛", with slightly heavier lines every inch, or every eight squares, vertically and horizontally. Art supply stores sell grid sheets.

FROG PATTERN ENLARGED.
To double the size of the little frog, start by making an outline tracing of the original design. If you are working with an original painting or photograph, this is the time to simplify the design into an uncomplicated and continuous outline. It must be continuous when you cut it out of veneer.

Next, place the celluloid grid sheet under the frog tracing (Figure 16) and fix both elements with tape to prevent slipping. Notice that the grid sheet extends under the area where the large frog pattern will be drawn. For working ease, draw pencil lines on the tracing paper on every

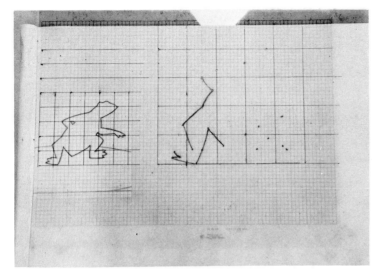

Figure 16. Celluloid grid laid beneath tracing paper simplifies graph-square method of enlarging or reducing a design.

fourth grid line over the little frog and every eighth grid line over the pattern area.

Plot the enlarged outline by making pencil dots where the outline of the frog touches or crosses a grid line. Count two grid squares on the pattern graph for one grid square of the original. Connect the dots freehand or with a French curve (Figure 17). Study the curves of the original frog each time you connect dots for the enlarged frog pattern. With your finished full-size pattern on tracing paper, you can turn the pattern over to reverse the direction of the frog required for "First Swimming Lesson" in Chapter 14.

HOW TO REVERSE A DESIGN. There are times when you need a reverse pattern. When developing your own designs, you may have a drawing of a frog jumping to the right. You want a second frog jumping left, toward your first frog. Again, as you become involved in marquetry, you will find that one of the conventional mar-

quetry systems starts with a reversed pattern.

Here is a simple way to reverse a design. First, place a sheet of carbon paper on your worktable, carbon side up. Put a sheet of white paper over the carbon. Next, put your design on top, design up. With stylus or sharp pencil, trace your original design. A reverse pattern will appear on the underside of the white paper.

HOW TO DRAW SYMMETRICAL SHAPES. When you are developing your own symmetrical design, a vase to hold roses for instance, this trick assures symmetry. On tracing paper draw a straight vertical line longer than the required height of the vase. This line becomes the centerline of the design. On one side of the line draw an outline of the vase, correcting it until you are satisfied with it. Lay this half-pattern on the veneer; trace first the centerline and then the outline. Turn the pattern over, line up the centerlines, and trace the second half of the subject. The sides will be identical since they came from one outline.

Figure 17. Dots made on enlargement where frog outline crosses a grid line are now connected with aid of French curve.

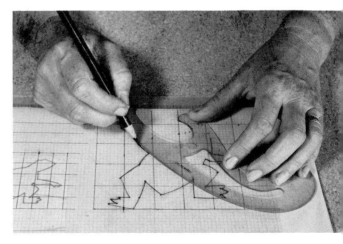

CHAPTER 5

Preparing Work Patterns

All one-piece designs in this book are ready to use without breakup. The "Bird in Flight" (Figure 18) is ready for transfer to a piece of tracing paper, which in turn will be traced on veneer for knife-cutting. The tracing paper serves as your work pattern.

For a more challenging exercise still requiring only one-piece patterns, you could make one larger and one smaller pattern of flying birds and arrange all three of them in a grouping on a mounting panel which has been veneered with gumwood. You might call it "Thunderhead" because it resembles flying birds against a thunderous sky.

Two-piece designs and other multiple-part designs generally require pattern breakup. When parts are layered as in the elephant design (Figure 19), where the head and trunk must be cut from one kind

Figure 18. A work pattern for simple one-piece designs like "Bird in Flight" can be made by tracing this outline or having a photocopy made of the page. Either method gives you a work pattern for knife-cutting or saw-cutting.

Figure 19. Elephant design requires pattern breakup. Head/trunk makes one work pattern, body makes the second work pattern. This is a two-piece layered cutout.

of veneer and the body cut from a contrasting veneer, you must break up the design into two work patterns.

Some two-piece designs with no layered parts still require pattern breakup. An example is "Bighorn I" (Figure 20). This design is so simple that, for knife-cutting, one pattern suffices. First, you use it to trace the animal on walnut; next, you use it to trace the rock on zebrano. For saw-cutting, you need two separate work patterns.

A wild rose composition consisting of three different sizes of pink flowers, numerous shapes and sizes of dark green leaves, and several dark stems breaks into three parts, one for each color. Pattern breakup is shown on saw pads (Figure 21), but the breakup would be the same for knife-cutting.

When you examine other saw pads in

later chapters, you will see that your cutting technique can sometimes eliminate pattern breakup. The mixed saw pad system, for example, can reduce breakup to a minimum.

Each design and each technique for cutting it are the factors that determine pattern breakup. Your own experience with veneers will guide you, and you will soon realize that most designs can be handled in a number of ways.

For a more complicated assignment, consider the multiple-part design of "Reclin-

Figure 20. "Bighorn I" is a two-piece design with adjoining parts, no layered parts. One work pattern serves for knife-cutting. Two separated work patterns are needed for saw-cutting.

Figure 21. Wild rose design of flowers, stems, and leaves breaks into three parts, one for each color of wood required. Saw pad method.

ing Lion" (Figure 22). Woods used in the lion scene are: butternut for legs, back patch, and flank; walnut for rock; mahogany for lion's body; and sycamore for face and muzzle. Using these woods, make separate pieces of all parts (Figure 23). Cut good joints for the rock and the lion and for the lion's patch. (See Chapter 7 for full instructions.) The rest of the cutting is easy because the parts are overlaid and do not require fitting (Figure 24).

There is another pattern breakup trick to be learned from the lion. To minimize intricate fitting, make the patch an overlay instead of an inset simply by running the lion's body underneath the patch area from rump to head. In the beginning, when you are using the knife-cutting method, avoid fitted insets and make overlays of as many parts as possible. For saw-cutting you should use the mixed saw pad method.

WORK PATTERNS. After you decide how you will break up a pattern for cutting, the

Figure 22. "Reclining Lion" presents several options for pattern breakup. A combination of layering and insetting was used. For knife-cutting, make separate work patterns for each different wood. Fill in your own line for the bottom of the lion's body. Printed patterns with all such lines would be totally confusing.

Figure 23. Cutout parts show that patch on body was inset, while the other parts were layered.

Figure 24. Color and figure of the assembled veneer parts create contrasting features of the lion.

next step is to prepare a work pattern. If you decide to knife-cut a particular part, use a tissue tracing or a photocopy of the part. Through black carbon paper (not blue because it smudges), trace the outline onto veneer. It is not practical to paste patterns onto veneer for knife-cutting.

If you plan to saw-cut a part, attach the appropriate piece of pattern on the top saw pad using rubber cement or a wax rubbing stick.

Photocopies are highly recommended as work patterns, because they are more accurate than pencil tracings. The lines are clear and easy to follow. And if you work with more than one, as you generally must do, they are identical, whereas no two tracings of the same design would match exactly.

CHAPTER 6

Selecting Veneers for Cutouts

Until you have examined forty or more kinds of what are known as exotic veneers you will have a hard time visualizing the large variety of colors and figure patterns available for your cutouts. Even when you know veneers well you will do better if you have samples in front of you to hold against the pattern while selecting.

The two guiding principles of selection are appropriateness to the design and color/figure contrast. By appropriateness we mean, for example, that reddish veneer makes an acceptable bird, but a red elephant would be a sorry-looking creature. For the bird, consider lacewood, a speckled figure sprinkled over a background of pinkish brown. It makes a handsome bird. For the elephant, try walnut, Oriental wood, or paldao—all are in the grayish brown color range with minimal figure. For a lion or a tiger, consider silky, golden satinwood or peroba, mottle figure.

Contrast between adjoining parts of a cutout is virtually mandatory. Without contrast, the parts fuse together instead of defining each shape or detail. Color creates contrast and so does figure pattern. A little trick to keep in mind is that just the act of turning veneer so that the figure pattern runs at right angles to an adjoining area of

the same kind of veneer can create a surprising amount of contrast without making the design as busy as changing colors would. Remember that you are painting a picture with woods and that you lack the artist's freedom to use shading and shadows for definition. This limitation makes you have to be more thoughtful in veneer selection.

When selecting veneers for various parts of the cutout, keep in mind the background. Contrast between the design and the background is equally vital. The background can too easily become a distracting feature in the picture. An example of appropriate use of background veneers is illustrated in the three-piece background for "Discovery of America" (Figure 25). The upper section of the veneered panel represents sky at night. In the sky there is a bright moon made of pale gold avodire, and there are ships and trees against the sky. Contrast was achieved by making the upper section the most striking color, dark purplish brown East Indian rosewood. For the moon-bright ocean, a piece of tamo ash with figure like gentle ocean waves was used. The light brown mahogany ships stand out against sky and ocean. The Island of San Salvador is the land in the

Figure 25. Select background veneers that express the scene. For "Discovery of America," dark rosewood represents the night sky, wavy tamo ash is the ocean, and light brown, striped Oriental wood is the tide-marked sandy beach of the island.

foreground. Grayish brown, earth-colored Oriental wood provided color contrast and just enough figure pattern to suggest tide marks on a sandy beach. Tamo ash was pieced at the right because the choice section of veneer was too short. The joint was made where a tree trunk, to be overlaid, would hide the joint.

There are times when the limited selection of veneers on hand requires compromise, but until you have switched available pieces back and forth, don't give in to it.

Avoid monotony. Many natural woods

are in the brown/tan color range, and designs can become monotonous using woods in only these colors. Changing figure direction is one way to create contrast. Oak, for example, looks quite different if you run the grain horizontally in one area and diagonally or vertically in the next piece. Another technique is to separate areas of similar tone with a bright, strong color. Use reddish padauk, for instance, between two browns, or orange-and-black Brazilian rosewood. Make constant use of texture. African cherry, deep reddish brown, has a

Figure 26. Make a cardboard viewer to move around on veneer until you find the best area for expressing the design. Without the viewer the fortunately located knot might have gone unnoticed.

silky sheen. Chinawood has a rough texture. Golden satinwood reflects a wavy pattern of light. Burls give animals a rough hide. Mix color, figure, and texture to define and separate the elements of your design, and you will make your wood pictures visually alive.

Make a viewer. After you have chosen the kind of veneer you want for a part of the design, narrow down your choice to a specific part of the veneer sheet. The best way is to make a simple cardboard viewer (Figure 26). Trace the work pattern onto a manila file folder. Cut out the outline with a knife, leaving a hole in the folder. It's a viewer, not a template, so there's no need for perfection. Move the viewer around on the veneer until you are satisfied with the direction of figure. Twist the viewer to the right, to the left, and try both sides of the veneer sheet. With viewer in place where you think you like the figure, hold veneer and viewer vertically to see it as it will be in the finished plaque. Light reflection is always better in one position.

You can make your viewer—that is, the

Figure 27. Cut your working squares of veneer from larger sheets with a veneer saw. It cuts straighter than a knife. This example is sapele.

outside square of the cardboard—the overall size of the saw pad. Then you can run a pencil around the outside edge of the viewer, and this line becomes your guide for cutting the sheet of veneer. By cutting the veneer on the guideline, you automatically maintain the correct direction of figure for the saw pad.

GETTING OUT THE VENEER. A veneer saw is the best tool for cutting a sheet of veneer (Figure 27). You can do it with a knife, but a stubborn figure sometimes pulls the knife away from the straightedge no matter what care you take.

When you cut with the saw, run it against a metal straightedge, which should be held very firmly to prevent slippage. Use the finer of the two sets of teeth. Start at the farthest edge of veneer and draw the saw toward you with only moderate pressure. Lift it as you approach the edge nearest you. Do not cut outward across an edge. Take several passes with the saw. Never try to cut through in fewer than about three passes. Some tough veneers take more. Draw the saw along slowly to avoid having it jump the straightedge toward your fingers or run away in the other direction across the veneer. Turn the veneer sheet around and gently finish the uncut edge. Never draw the saw across the edge nearest to you. If you do, the veneer may split. When cutting cross-grain be especially careful to avoid splitting edges.

If you are going to cut with a knife, particularly cross-grain, stick clear tape on the underside of the veneer, aligned with the cutting line. This precaution is more important with some veneers than with others. Experience is your only guide. Make a trial cut in a waste area if you are in doubt. Under-taping is not necessary when you cut with the veneer saw.

Here is another trick for cross-cutting. Keep it in mind when you are having chipping problems with a particular piece—crumbly burls, for example. Make a scoring cut with the veneer saw and then finish cutting with your knife. The saw kerf guides the knife and keeps it from being pulled out of line by tough grain. The saw/knife combination used in this way sometimes makes a cleaner cut than any other cross-cutting method.

Every working piece of veneer you get out should be oversize. Allow 1″ margin at every edge of the piece from which you

will cut a design part. The edges of intricate shapes near the edge of the veneer are more likely to split than are bold shapes.

For saw pads and for knife-cutting, the pieces of veneer do not have to have perfect right-angled corners. These pieces are cut oversize. Veneer you cut for mounting panels is cut with less margin for trimming, usually ³/₁₆″; and a margin of only ³/₁₆″ at each edge of a 9″ x 11″ panel does not allow for sloppy gluing. When you need square pieces to fit into a square layout, such as the modern art tray in Chapter 14, you will find that perfect squares are vital.

The 24″ steel square is the best tool for accurate layout of veneer squares which are too large for your 12″ square. It is also best for checking squareness of the piece you have cut.

Checking small pieces for right angles is easier with the small combination square, bought for very little from a bargain box at a lumberyard. When using the square, hold the veneer tightly in place and look for spots around the edges where light may show through and where sanding is needed.

CHAPTER 7

Knife-Cutting Techniques

Each of the four methods of cutting veneer designs has its advantages and its shortcomings. Knife-cutting and razor-cutting are the easiest to prepare for: trace a work pattern onto veneer and you are ready to cut. In the hands of an expert, the knife can cut close-fitting joints, but beginners without artistic talent are not likely to cut very good joints initially. For its house manners, the knife method has strong supporters. It is the cleanest: no sawdust on the rug. And it is quiet: no sawing noise or pulsating motor to disturb the family.

CUTTING CHARACTERISTICS OF VENEERS.

The $1/40''$ veneers are easier to cut with a knife, but they require more care in handling than heavier woods, both before and after cutting. The standard thickness of $1/28''$, by far the largest group of veneers available, cuts cleanly with a knife but takes longer to cut than $1/40''$ veneers.

A few varieties of $1/28''$ are difficult to cut with a knife. Bubinga, ebony, satinwood, and oak are tough, especially cross-grain. Most dyed veneers are more brittle than natural varieties. They are easier to cut cross-grain than with-grain. With-grain they stubbornly pull the knife away from the cutting line. Cutting difficulty isn't rea-

son enough to avoid these veneers, however. They are worth the extra time and patience. You can minimize knife-cutting of the tough ones by using the veneer saw wherever the design line is straight and of course when getting out a work-size sheet of veneer from a large sheet.

TRACING THE PATTERN ON VENEER.

If your design is composed of more than one kind of veneer, as most designs are, obviously you must make each piece separately. Trace your work pattern of one element through black carbon paper onto the sheet of veneer.

Practically all cutting in veneer craft is done from the face side of the veneer, but cutting from the back is preferred where close-fitting joints are involved, such as in marquetry pictures. The point of the knife coming through the underside cuts a finer line than does the broadening blade, which leaves a wider, slightly beveled cut-line on the side you are cutting from. When you use this marquetry trick, be sure to turn your pattern over before tracing it onto the back of the veneer sheet.

TAPING THE BACK.

If you have never before cut the kind of wood you are working with, try cutting a curve and a straight line in waste area. If the wood splinters along the knife line when you are cutting crossgrain, or if it pulls the knife stubbornly with the grain, it is advisable to lay clear tape on the back of the wood, beneath the cutting line. This helps immeasurably in preventing a faulty cut. It is a nuisance to remove because it must be picked off carefully and pulled slowly away from the veneer, but it is an important safeguard. A knife is the best instrument for starting to peel off used tape.

CARDBOARD TEMPLATES. When duplicate pieces are needed to compose a design, cardboard templates are your best aid. They assure identical parts and they prevent carbon smudges that are hard to remove from light-colored veneer. Make templates of clean-cutting single-weight bristol drawing board, or use a manila file

Figure 28. An intricate cardboard template for a rose of red maple burl serves also as a viewer for locating best wood figure. A separate template for each petal would be a safer method for beginner.

folder, which is cheaper and works just as well. Trace your work pattern onto the cardboard and cut out the piece with a single-edge razor blade or craft knife. Smooth the cut edge with knife or sandpaper. Figure 28 is a highly sophisticated combination viewer and template for a rose to be made of red maple burl. The beginner will do better to cut a separate template for each element of the flower.

Lay the cardboard template on the veneer. Fix its position with snips of tape. Trace around it with a sharp pencil. Move only one piece of tape out of the way at a time. It may be tempting to knife-score around the template to incise a track-line, but your knife may nick the edge of your template and mar it.

VENEER TEMPLATES. When one veneer part fits into another in your design, the veneer template method is your best aid. After you have cut one part, use it as a template for marking the cutting line on the second part. Figure 29 shows a light green veneer frog laid in position on dark green veneer for the lily pad. Trace around the frog with a pencil or make a track-line with your knife. Move the frog out of the way and knife-cut the lily pad. Take care to cut accurately, and the fit will be perfect.

SPECIALTY TEMPLATES. Anything you can find that will guide your knife in making a first track-line is worth trying. You can use a French curve (being careful to prevent nicks in the celluloid) or an empty pill vial for common curves or circles.

USING KNIFE AND STRAIGHTEDGE. For straight cuts, these tools work well together. Use them on two pieces of veneer when you need a good straight joint be-

Figure 29. One cut part laid on veneer for a joining part makes the best template of all. Frog cutout is to be set into oval lily pad.

point toward the mass. Do not run your knife outward toward a point. This work rule can make for awkward cutting positions unless you can move your work easily. Tape the veneer to a small, swiveling workboard. This device moves the work constantly to the best cutting position (Figure 31).

Here are the most important rules to follow for successful knife-cutting of veneers:

1. Change to a fresh blade every time you start a new project, and change again partway through if you are required to cut delicate parts and have been using the old blade for an hour or so. The sensible way to make this exchange is to have several knives in your work kit. This allows you to

tween two cutout parts. Lay one sheet of veneer on top of the other, cut through both pieces without shifting straightedge or veneers. Even if the knife wiggles, the cuts will be identical, and the two pieces will fit perfectly. Figure 30 shows how the straightedge protects the veneer part needed for a cutout. Always place the straightedge where it protects the working part from a slip of the knife.

CUTTING TINY PARTS. When cutting out small parts, you need a piece large enough to hold firmly. Never cut tiny parts from an edge of the veneer. Leave at least ½" at each edge.

CUTTING INTRICATE PARTS. When cutting designs with points, cut from the

Figure 30. Where you have a choice, use your straightedge as a veneer protector, laying it over the part you will use. If knife slips, it does so in the waste area.

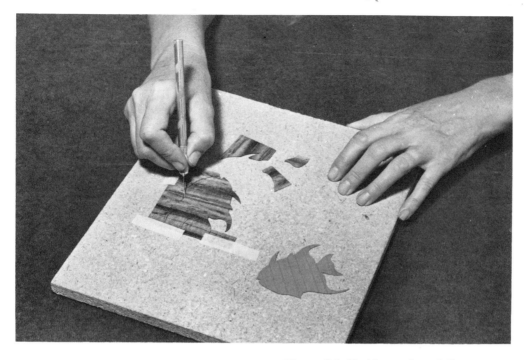

Figure 31. Knife-cutting delicate parts is always done from several directions to avoid breakage. Tape such parts to small workboard which you can swivel easily into best cutting position.

change quickly and keep the used blade for less delicate work.

2. Make a well-defined, single-line tracing of the pattern onto the veneer; that is, pencil around the pattern line once, instead of going around two or three times to fill it or improve a badly drawn line.

3. Make a light first cut as a track-line to guide the knife during second and third cuts. Never attempt to cut through the veneer on the first cut.

4. Go slowly, just as slowly as you can move the knife. When the knife sticks, as it will, don't press harder. Do just the opposite. Lift the knife slightly to release it, then continue with lighter pressure.

5. Cut with the point of your knife. Hold the knife sufficiently upright to press the point to the cutting line.

6. Over-cut at the starting point. Wherever it is practical and does not increase risk of splitting a nearby design, start the point of your knife a little beyond the actual guideline. This practice prevents points and corners of a design from breaking, and it makes a cleaner point.

7. Avoid little jabbing, hacking cuts with the knife. It slivers the wood on both sides of the line. Make firm, deliberate movements, always in the same track-line.

8. Tape intricate cutouts to a small, swiveling workboard. Pivot the work for the best light and to avoid awkward cutting positions that cause sloppy cutting. Pivot the board as you cut around a curve. If the knife sticks badly in one stubborn spot of especially tough grain, turn the board and cut into the spot from the opposite direction.

9. When the cut is deep into the veneer, the knife sticks frequently. Hold the veneer down with a fingertip close to the side of the knife blade.

10. Have ½″ snips of clear tape ready to stick behind your knife-cut where you see the veneer lifting and therefore know that the cut is all the way through.

11. When cutting around a tight curve, roll the knife in your fingers. This practice avoids jerky changes of direction made with the wrist or arm.

12. Be careful while making cuts along straight grain. Grain can pull your knife off the guideline before you know what's happening.

13. When cutting cross-grain, especially at a point where you meet a cut-line at an angle, watch out for the corner. It will split easily. To overcome this problem, some craftsmen lay clear tape on the opposite side of the veneer, directly under the cutting line.

RAZOR-CUTTING TECHNIQUES.

The single-edge razor blade with a heavy backbone is just as good a cutting tool as a craft knife. (Double-edge blades in holders are too flimsy for cutting veneer.) You use the razor blade in much the same way as the knife for the same cutting jobs, as it has a sharp, tapered tip. In fact, the tip is thinner than a craft-knife blade. Even with tape on your pressure finger, however, the razor is not as comfortable for prolonged use as the knife. Nor can it be sharpened satisfactorily by home methods. But it does have two tips, and it is the lowest-priced tool you can buy.

Beginners find it a little harder to follow curving lines accurately with the razor blade until they have had experience with it. It seems to cut cleaner on $1/40″$ than on $1/28″$. With the thinner veneer and the heavier pressure you can put on the razor blade, you can normally go right through on the first cut. If you try the razor blade method, try it with extra pressure, going only once along a cutting line. With razor blade or knife, it is the second and later passes that deviate from the line and cause uneven edges. Skill comes more easily with the knife, but to see what practice can do, look at several examples in Chapter 14. "Discovery of America" and "Playful Panda" were cut with a razor blade.

CHISEL BLADE.

The knife that holds a pointed blade for cutting veneer also can take a chisel blade, shown elsewhere in the knife pot. The chisel blade is used for trimming off tiny projections or for cutting out a piece for the eye of a frog or the broken ear of a horse. It is better than a knife for such close work but should be used only for straight cuts. Use it by coming down straight on the veneer, bevel edge of the tool away from the piece you are saving. Rock it slightly. Press down hard. The waste piece will snap off and the cut will be clean. The chisel blade is also the best tool for cleanup. Use it to scrape off excess dried glue and to scrape over a filled joint when the filling mix has dried. Scraping dulls the chisel, but this is one tool that is very easy to sharpen.

SAFETY PRECAUTIONS.

Knives move easily in soft grain but stick occasionally in hard grain. As you pull harder, the knife can slip. Several hand tricks are helpful to know. Right-hand fingers sliding along the edge of a panel steady the knife and brake it to keep it from sliding out across the veneer or into the edge of the panel. Figure 32 shows a wood-carver's way of braking the knife hand with a thumb behind the chuck. For panel trimming the free hand must keep the panel from shifting and be ready to brake the knife hand (Figure 33). You need two positions because you should cut from each corner toward the center.

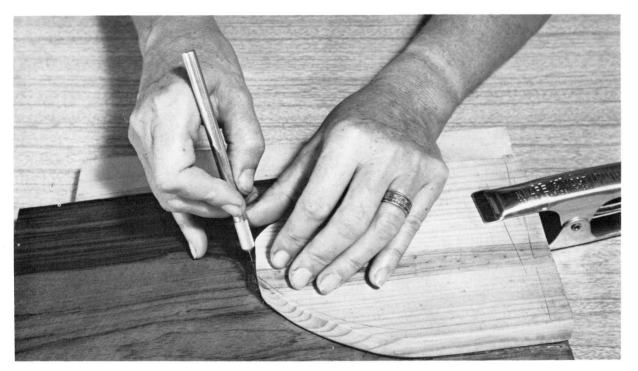

Figure 32. Knife-safety work habits should be thoughtfully figured out. Wood-carvers use hand or thumb, whichever fits the job, to brake the forward pull of the knife.

Everyone eventually works out his own braking systems.

In some illustrations you will see a thermos cork on the workboard. This is another safety device. Where work space is limited, it substitutes for the knife pot. Stick the knife point into the larger end of the cork when not cutting. Never allow a knife to roll around on your workboard.

Figure 33. Holding positions when trimming overhang from mounting panels must be worked out by trial. Here the left hand, with fingers back from path of knife, brakes thrust of panel.

CHAPTER 8

Saw-Cutting Techniques

The first fret saw on record appeared in 1562. The first useful jig saw, operated by foot power, was invented in 1780. By the 1800s, various styles of fret saw appeared in workshops of American craftsmen. Their prevalence paralleled important advances in veneer manufacture. Power tools, driven by water power and later by steam, were invented and were soon adapted to the process of sawing veneers into sheets. While these veneers were more uniform, they still were relatively thick, seldom less than $1/8''$. They were heavy enough to be cut into intricate designs for inlay and marquetry without using security backing.

Today, veneers are knife-sliced so thin that they no longer can be cut without backing. The saw pad was, therefore, an invention of necessity. It started as a device to prevent fragile veneers from being split and chipped by action of the saw. No better system has replaced it as a safety measure. But the saw pad has also become extremely useful in other ways. It is such a versatile device that you, too, will undoubtedly improvise adaptions beyond the basic uses demonstrated in this chapter.

A simple description of a saw pad is that it is a sandwich—fragile veneers layered between two thicker pieces of wood and bound together at all edges. The top and bottom pieces are called blinds, presumably because they shield the veneer visually. A pattern is transferred to the top blind, and the entire saw pad is cut to the outline of the pattern. The blinds are then discarded.

The primary requirement of the saw pad method is a fret saw or a jig saw. When a fret saw is used, a bird's-mouth saw table is needed. Other essentials are: a small drill, masking tape, clear tape, and rubber cement. A detailed discussion of tools and saw pad materials appears in Chapter 3.

Before you choose the saw pad method from among the many variations open to you, inspect the design and think the problem all the way through to the assembly of parts. Choose the method that best fits the major parts of a design. For example, know in advance how every part would come out of the pad. Often two types of saw pads are better for color contrast or for economy of materials than a single pad. A combination of saw and knife methods may be the simplest technique. No single saw pad system applies to all veneer craft designs.

Saw pads for one-piece designs are the simplest. "Birds in Flight" is a design con-

Figure 34. The simplest saw pad contains one sheet of lacewood for one-piece designs.

sisting of three birds of varying sizes, drawn at different angles of flight (full-size pattern in Chapter 14). Two design factors, size and angle, will create an illusion of distance when you assemble the three cutouts on a mounting panel. The simple saw pad for these birds (Figure 34) has all three patterns cut apart and pasted on the top blind about as close together as is practical. Between the blinds, the pad is layered with one sheet of lacewood. You can see that this design could have been cut with your craft knife with about the same result. The only reason for choosing the saw pad method for this simple design is personal preference for sawing.

MULTIPLE SAW PADS. While you are sawing out one copy of a design, you can just as easily cut multiples. From the "Flying Angel" pad, two angels can be cut (Figure 35). It is entirely practical to cut even more, simply by layering the pad with more squares of satinwood veneer, up to about five. Pads with more than five layers would tend to break more saw blades than the higher production is worth. That you can cut two to five angels at one time from one saw pad proves the value of the saw pad as a time-saver. You cannot, for example, knife-cut multiple angels as fast as you can saw one pattern on a saw pad.

MIXED SAW PAD. The lion was cut in one saw pad. His mane is Brazilian rosewood; his head is peroba, matching his silky peroba body (Figure 36). When I studied the design for this lion ("Lion's Pride," Chapter 14), two alternative production methods were considered. First, the lion could be cut as one complete animal, and the mane could be cut separately and applied as an overlay. This could have been carried out with knife or saw. The overlay is the wisest method if you do not own a fret saw, because it involves the least amount of close fitting.

The second method of production, insetting the mane between head and body, was chosen because I decided it would look better. For insetting, use the mixed pad system. It is the easiest. Two woods are inserted in one saw pad. Interlocking cuts are made with a single pass of the saw be-

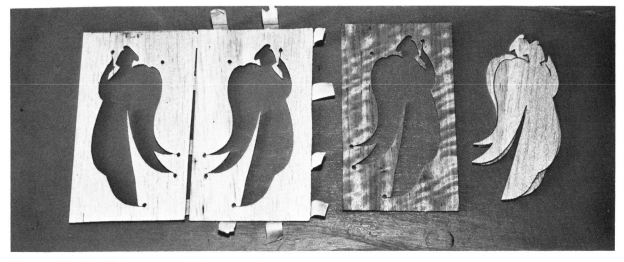

Figure 35. Multiple saw pad for angels was layered with two sheets of satinwood. Opened pad shows top and bottom blinds, waste satinwood sheets, and two complete angels.

tween mane and head, another between body and mane. This produces perfect-fitting joints, because you make only one cut along one pattern line.

In the mixed pad system, the two woods layered in the saw pad would be one full sheet of peroba and one full sheet of rosewood. This combination of two full sheets of veneer would produce two complete lions in a mixed assembly; that is, one lion with rosewood mane, peroba head and body, as illustrated; and one lion with peroba mane, rosewood head and body. The second combination in this case is not very lionlike and should probably be discarded. However, in many other examples of mixed pads you will see that the second complete assembly is just as attractive as the first. An example is seen in "Prehistoric America" where Stegosaurus, the creature with the sawtooth back plate, was produced in duplicate and assembled with parts intermixed.

Knowing in advance that the second complete lion would be inappropriate, I chose still another variation of the saw pad system—the patch pad method.

PATCH PAD. Layering the lion saw pad in the obvious way with two full sheets of

Figure 36. Mixed saw pad for lion held two veneers, rosewood and peroba. One cutting operation produced closely interlocking parts for two complete lions. Combination of peroba head/body and rosewood mane is shown.

Figure 37. Patch pad offers a way to economize on precious veneer and to utilize small leftovers. Common poplar is patched to rosewood to fill out a full sheet for the pad. Rosewood makes the lion's mane, and poplar becomes waste.

veneer would have been something of a waste of rosewood. The decision was made to patch-pad rosewood (Figure 37). Notice that only a small piece of rosewood, cut at the desired angle of veneer figure for the mane, was patched to a piece of inexpensive poplar which will become waste. Filling out the sheet with poplar was necessary for a smooth, level pad. The patch pad method is useful for economizing valuable veneer. It is useful, also, for salvaging irregular pieces of veneer.

In marquetry you will often find a saw pad layered with four or five patch sheets so skillfully arranged that an amazingly small amount of veneer is wasted.

The larger your saw pad, the more welcome the patch system becomes. An example of patch pad economy is shown in the construction method for a two-piece veneer background for a fairly large mounting panel (Figure 38). I chose two prized sheets of veneer: curly maple for the sky, green poplar burl for the ocean. By filling out the required sheet with a large common poplar patch, I was able to use only a small sheet of precious poplar burl. The lower section of the curly maple could have been patched, but here the small waste was tolerated.

Another example of a patch pad shows how the saw pad system can produce inter-

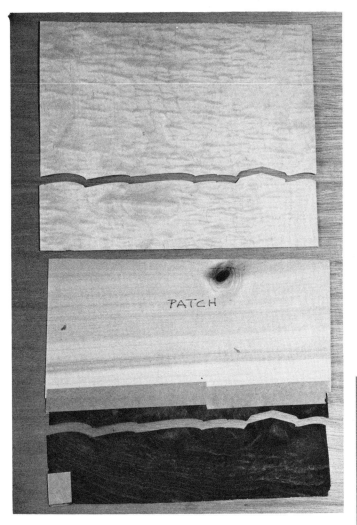

Figure 38. Example of major patch pad economy and mixed pad technique. Without patch, larger piece of poplar burl would be needed, and without cutting curly maple sky and burl ocean in one pad, the intricate joint would have been less accurate.

esting background assemblies for your mounting panels. "Mexico" (Chapter 14) has a five-piece veneer assembly. Each adjoining area is a different veneer, but only three kinds of veneer are used, and only two full sheets of veneer went into the pad.

The upper one-third of sheet I is primavera. The lower two-thirds is butternut. The two kinds are taped together. The upper half of sheet II is gumwood; the lower half is primavera. Numbers on the pad show what is to be cut from each section (Figure 39): sky, primavera; mountain, gumwood; field, butternut; road, primavera; foreground, butternut.

While it may sound complicated, this mixed/patch pad is actually fairly simple. Notice, for instance, that sheet I yields the sky for the top element of the mounting panel. Sheet II yields the next element, the mountain. Sheet I next yields the field. Sheet II, the road. Sheet I, the foreground. Every other piece is usable. Every other piece is waste.

Had it not been for the patch pad system, I could not use gumwood. Since the grain runs horizontally across the as-

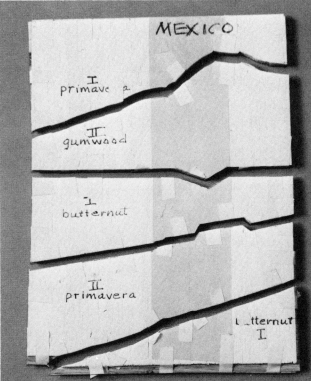

Figure 39. Large mixed pad produces interesting five-piece veneer assembly for "Mexico" mounting panel.

sembly, to fill the pad with full sheets of each of three veneers would require a sheet of gumwood at least 12″ wide, measured cross-grain. It isn't available that wide. The choice was either to patch the gumwood sheet, or use a different veneer. There is no problem in obtaining wide primavera and butternut.

The other reason for selecting the pad system is nearly always the same—perfection. Every joint fits accurately because only one saw cut is made for joining pieces.

COMPLETE-PICTURE PAD. Perhaps the ultimate use of the saw pad is to layer it with all woods needed in a design (Figure 40). If you cement the entire pattern on the top blind and saw-cut along all pattern lines, the yield is barely believable. Instead of one cutout, you now have four complete, intermixed cutouts; that is, four copies of every piece. If you have chosen

Figure 40. Layered with four different veneers, the "Leaping Salmon" saw pad will produce four complete salmon with mixed colors. Example demonstrates how a single saw pad can produce complete pictures.

woods having only subtle color differences, the four sets will all be attractive combinations.

OPEN PAD METHOD. Core assemblies (stable material veneered on both sides) like the turtle puzzle, chessmen, and trapeze aerialists (all in Chapter 14), are strong enough for saw-cutting with only a bottom blind. This is the open pad method. Cement the pattern directly on the face veneer. To avoid rubber-cement stain on the veneer, apply cement around the perimeter of the pattern where cement will smear only waste areas of the veneer.

Some craftsmen use the open pad method when they are in a hurry for a replacement part. They tape a single piece of veneer to a bottom blind, trace or paste a pattern on the veneer, and saw it to shape. This risky practice can be done for only small, compact designs. The only safeguard when sawing is to hold the veneer and pad down on the saw table and apply hard finger pressure very close to the saw blade.

SAW PAD CONSTRUCTION. Top and bottom blinds of saw pads prevent veneer breakage. The size and delicacy of the design are the factors to weigh when deciding on blind material. Balsa is suitable for most pads up to about 6″ square. Larger pads should be constructed of ⅛″ poplar for the bottom blind and either ¹/₂₈″ poplar or balsa for the top blind. Two blinds of the heavy poplar make sawing difficult.

Begin building the saw pad with the top blind. Cut your work pattern reasonably close to the outline. Knife-cut a balsa blind with an oversize allowance of ¾″ to 1″ at all edges, and cement pattern to top blind. Lay the blind onto each large veneer sheet, trace and cut out the veneer worksheets. Then cut the bottom blind to the same size. Heavy poplar is too thick for knife-cutting, so you'll have to use a dovetail saw or some other saw.

To bind the pad tightly together, use masking tape, not clear tape. Follow the professional's trick of rolling a stream of tape across your cutting board and slitting it in half-a-dozen places to produce convenient lengths. Lift a corner of each piece with a knife so it will be easy to pick up. This practice saves time and keeps scissors from getting gummed up. To bind the saw pad edges, place each snip of tape on the design side of the pad where it doesn't cover pattern lines. Start three or four pieces across one long edge, turn the pad over, pull the tape very tight, and press it down. Add more tape to bind the pad firmly around all edges.

REINFORCING THE PAD.
Large pads tend to flop up and down in central areas when you are sawing. To avoid this, you can spot-glue veneer layers within the pad and spot-glue veneer to inside surfaces of blinds before binding the pad. Of course, you must be extremely careful to spot-glue pad ingredients only in waste areas.

Professional inlayers customarily use nails to reinforce saw pads. A No. 19 headed nail ½" long is satisfactory. Drive nails in waste areas only. Snip the points that come through the other side and file snaggy points so that there will be nothing to catch on your saw table.

When the pad is secure, drill a few starting holes in waste areas and saw-cut a few pattern lines to pre-considered stopping points. You have to stop frequently to tape the saw kerf and to start the saw at another point of the pattern. While stopped, you can drill a few more starting holes.

This cutting procedure requires a cut-

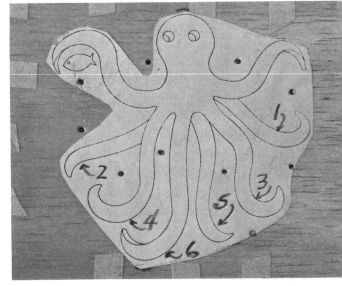

Figure 41. Preserve pad stability as long as possible by following an alternating sawing sequence, as suggested for octopus.

ting strategy for the entire pattern. Consider the octopus, a design with many extending, fragile parts (Figure 41). Numbers on the pattern indicate cutting sequence. Notice that only every other line for tentacles is cut at first so as to keep the pad stable for as long as possible. The best rule is to cut interior lines and far-separated lines before you cut perimeter lines and nearby lines.

Poorly located starting holes require unnecessary pad cutting which contributes to a floppy pad. Often you can drill starting holes near pointed ends of pattern lines in such a location that one hole gives you two fresh starts, one to the left and one to the right. Drill as few starting holes as you can. Never drill until you have double-checked the location. It is easy to hurriedly drill a damaging hole in a usable area.

Threading the fret saw: A few tips on saw blade installation will save you a lot of trouble figuring it out for yourself. The two types of fret saws illustrated are

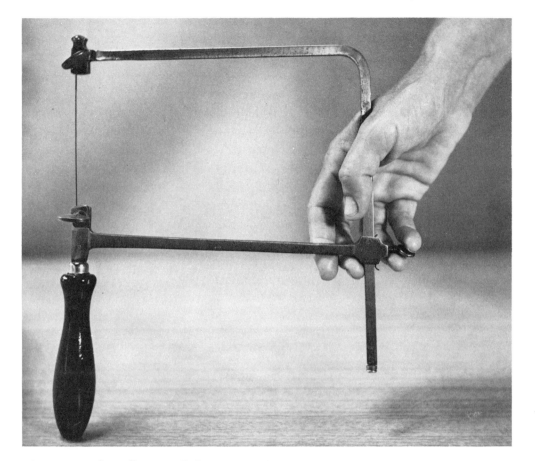

Figure 42. Threading small fret saw is demonstrated without saw pad. Notice finger positions of right hand for lifting lower arm of saw frame to bring lower chuck to right height for engaging blade. After chuck has been tightened, use right hand to depress the lower arm to increase blade tension.

threaded differently because of construction differences. The small saw is easiest to thread. Start by raising the upper sliding arm quite high, far from the lower chuck. Tighten the saw blade in the upper chuck with teeth forward and pointing down. Hold the dangling saw blade over the starting hole in the saw pad. Drop it through the hole. Engaging the lower chuck is tricky until you know how. As in Figure 42, use the right hand to lift the lower arm along the rear post until the lower end of

the blade can be guided into the lower chuck and tightened with the left hand. Next, with the right hand, depress the lower arm and twist the thumbscrew tight. This increases tension of the saw blade. You want the blade quite tight.

The large fret saw, a necessity for work over 9″ square, has no sliding arm. It relies on spring tension of the two long steel arms. This saw will not take a blade shorter than 5″. Start threading by engaging the blade in the upper chuck. Because the lower arm will not drop down out of the way, you can rather easily snap a blade while trying to thread it through a starting hole in the pad. The best preventive measure is to hold pad and saw at a sharp angle while threading. This scheme entails a minimum of blade-flexing while you are starting the blade in the hole. Straighten the saw upright and drop the blade through the hole. Grip the saw frame as shown and pull it together as much as you can with the right hand while you guide the blade into the lower chuck and tighten the thumbscrew (Figure 43). Here, too, you want a tight blade.

Blades are discussed in Chapter 3 along with more details about tools and equipment for sawing. The best blade for the newcomer is the sturdy 6″ length. This is the coarsest you can use. In the beginning, you will break a few of these fairly tough blades, but you will soon develop the skill you need to use fine blades. When you do, choose as fine a blade as you can get by with, and make your selection on the basis of the intricacy of the design and of the contents and thickness of the saw pad. Work experience is the only teacher. Some craftsmen break blades frequently. Some rarely break a blade.

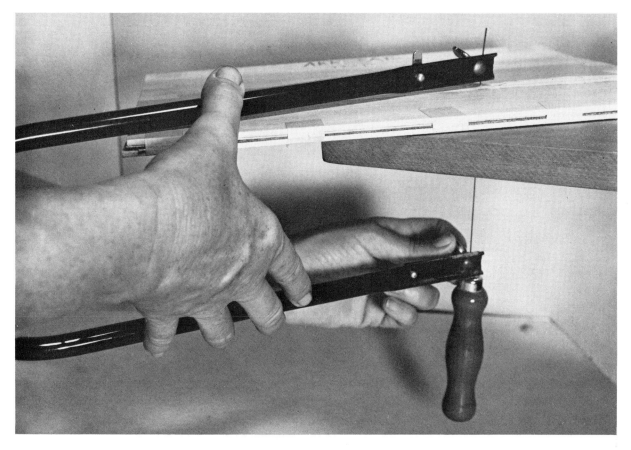

Figure 43. To engage blade in lower chuck, squeeze saw frame hard while you twist thumbscrew of lower chuck. Release grip, and flexible frame automatically creates blade tension.

Figure 44. Saw table overextends worktable when clamped as shown. Notch and hole provide enough space for saw blade to work up and down while saw pad is firmly supported on table.

SAW TABLE. Work must be supported on a wooden, expendable table called a bird's-mouth. The commercial variety (Figure 44) is bought with its own clamp for attaching the saw table firmly to a worktable. The homemade variety is a piece of ¾″ pine. The V-notch and hole permit the saw blade to be worked deep into the bird's-mouth so that the saw pad is well supported.

WORK-FEED. It is obvious that you saw an outline by working the saw up and down, cutting only on the down stroke because you installed the blade with teeth downward. The up stroke removes sawdust from the saw kerf. Blow it away as it accumulates so that it does not shield your pattern line. Work-feed means just that—feeding work into the saw. Keep your saw in one position, not swinging around curves. Move it steadily at all times and slowly until you have more skill. A stroke of 2″ is about right. While pumping the saw, use your left hand to guide the work toward you, paying close attention to the pattern line. Resist the dangerous temptation to push the saw into the work.

To round a curve, swing the saw pad slowly. To maneuver around a fairly sharp curve, slow down on the work-feed but keep pumping the saw. If the saw sticks when rounding a sharp turn, pushing will break it. Keep the saw in motion, but back up the work a tiny bit, and you will free the saw. Where intersecting lines meet at a very sharp inside corner, work to the corner, free the saw blade from the lower chuck, and remove the saw pad so gently that you will not snap the blade. Now insert the blade through another starting hole and come into the sharp corner from another direction.

You can overcut the converging lines forming an outside point of the design, but you must not overcut interior converging lines. This type of cut must be very precise to avoid conspicuous nicks in the finished cutout. When you play it too safe by not cutting fully into the corner and you find the cutout stuck when you open the pad, insert a piece of broken saw blade and work into the corner by hand-sawing. Normally only a few strokes of the blade are needed to free the cutout from the pad.

Keep the pad stable with tape. Have a number of snips of clear tape on a table edge nearby where you can reach them. As you saw along the pattern line, stop frequently to lay a small strip of tape across the saw kerf behind your saw blade. Do the same thing on the underside of the pad when you can reach without twisting the saw and breaking a blade. You can always tape underneath kerfs when you disengage the blade.

OPENING SAW PADS. Slit the masking tape along two sides and the bottom of the pad, leaving the *upper* edge hinged. Then you can either pry the cutout cautiously from its surrounding veneer waste or you can slide the entire veneer sheet, cutout and waste, onto a workboard, where the sections should fall apart with a little help from you. Sometimes this method requires slitting the top tape hinge to loosen the veneer. You should do whichever seems safer for a particular cutout. When you open pads containing nails, because of the intricacy of the design, remove the nails first. You can slip the point of a utility knife around and under the nail head and pry it up enough to get underneath the head with nippers. Pull all nails gently.

CHAPTER 9

Mounting Panels for Cutouts

The veneer parts you cut are too fragile for assembly on anything other than a smooth, solid surface. Never mount veneer parts on paper or cardboard if you expect to preserve the design. The wood would soon warp and split, even if the assembly was not damaged by handling. Infrequently there have been simple designs mounted on greeting cards, but they break, often before they are received and certainly shortly thereafter.

The sides and fronts of chests, cabinets, cupboards, and the flat panels of headboards and cribs are great places for applying veneer decorations, as most of these make good gluing surfaces. Clamping may present special problems, however, which you will have to work out. Wood-paneled walls are good gluing surfaces where vertical grooving is no handicap. One of the best panels in the modern home is the flat, hollow-core door. Plain, uninteresting, wasted space like this can be enlivened with a colorful pictorial cutout.

READY-MADE MOUNTING PANELS. The quickest way to provide yourself with plaque-style mounting panels for your cutouts is to buy plywood panels. Quarter-inch thickness is about right for designs up to 12″ x 24″. Suitable plywood comes veneered with choice wood on one side and common wood on the back. This is the cheapest and the best you need. Choice woods ordinarily available in the 12″ x 24″ size include walnut, mahogany, oak, maple, rosewood, cherry, and teak. Think in terms of color contrast with the cutout when you purchase plywood panels. Avoid fir plywood because of its uneven surface and distracting figure.

CUTTING PLYWOOD PANELS. Many of the designs you decide to make will not fit well on a stock panel bought from suppliers. You can cut the 12″ x 24″ panel into three panels 8″ x 12″, a very useful size. The problem is that the face veneer often gets chipped with the saw. The best way to minimize chipping is to cut a V-groove across the panel with your craft knife. Cut along the groove with a power table saw if you have access to one; if not, clamp a wooden straightedge to the panel and let it guide your saw as you cut along the V-groove. The best tool for the purpose is a backsaw or a dovetail saw (Figure 45).

Figure 45. Clamp a wooden fence across panel to guide dovetail saw along V-groove. The groove prevents saw from chipping face veneer.

MAKING MOUNTING PANELS. If you decide to make your own mounting panels for your cutout designs, you will want to apply an attractive veneer face to the panel front. You must also veneer the back to create balanced construction or the panel will warp. The back veneer can be a cheaper kind such as poplar, sycamore, or plain mahogany. The face veneer should be chosen with the color and figure of the cutout design in mind. Select a veneer that complements your picture. Avoid highly figured woods that detract from a design.

Quarter-inch tempered hardboard is suitable for mounting panels up to about 9" x 12". Larger sizes may warp, although I successfully use it for panels up to 12" x 24". It is thinner and lighter in weight than the next best choice, flakeboard, which is known in many lumberyards as particle board. The thinnest flakeboard you can use is ⅜". For panels larger

than about 9" x 12" make sure you get 45-lb. test or higher when you buy flakeboard. Your supplier can show you the test rating stamped on the board. Flakeboard is much heavier than hardboard and when used for wall plaques it may require larger wall fixtures. It is also more stable than hardboard. In sizes you will use, it will never warp, providing that you follow veneering instructions. Veneer the front with choice veneer and cover the back with any less valuable veneer. If the veneer you want to use is available in sheets large enough to cut a one-piece face, that is the easiest way to do it. Most of the pictorials in Chapter 14 were laid on mounting panels covered with a one-piece face. Other panels had two or more pieces joined in an attractive way. "Discovery of America" was laid on a three-piece face, "Mexico" on a five-piece face. In Chapter 8 you saw how this was accomplished.

Flakeboard is an excellent, porous sur-

Figure 46. Scratch hardboard panels to roughen surfaces for better glue bond.

face which bonds perfectly with glue. Hardboard is smooth and does not bond as well until you roughen the surface (Figure 46) with a knife. Scratch the edges lightly to avoid visible edge holes in the veneered panel.

PREPARING VENEER FOR PANEL. Before you apply glue to the panel you intend to cover with a one-piece face veneer, prepare the sheet of veneer properly. Cut it oversize, about ⅜″ wider and longer than the panel. This size gives you a welcome ³/₁₆″ margin of safety at each edge, should the panel or the veneer slip a trifle when being clamped. The margin also allows for accidental splitting of a corner when you are cutting the sheet and for a split edge caused by handling.

JOINING TWO SHEETS. There are times when you find a sheet of veneer that is the ideal color and figure for a background, but it is not wide enough for the mounting panel. It is probable that you bought two or more sheets, and, since veneers normally are sold in consecutive sheets, just as they were cut from the log, it is likely you have a matching pair. If so, you can join them together with gummed tape and glue down the assembly as a single sheet. This is an important procedure in general veneering and a useful technique to know.

First, you must cut a good joint. Open the two sheets as you open a book. What you see is called a matching pair, or a two-piece match. The two edges you intend to join are irregular. To cut them to fit well together, lay one sheet so that the joining edge slightly overlaps the second sheet. Hold a straightedge on top, back from the edge only far enough to remove the irregular edge. Cut along the straightedge with your veneer saw (Figure 47) cutting

Figure 47. Best joint is made by saw-cutting through both veneer sheets at one time, with top piece overlapping. This is one of the most important techniques in veneering. Demonstration pieces are satinwood.

through both sheets of veneer. Cutting the edges at one time this way makes a better joint than you could possibly make by cutting two edges separately.

To join the two sheets, hold them tightly together and lay paper tape down the joint (Figure 48). Turn the assembly over carefully, flex open the joint slightly, and squeeze glue into the open joint. Smeared glue is all right since this is the side you will glue down when you lay the assembled two-piece match on your mounting panel. Tape comes off easily when the panel comes out of clamps or weights.

MULTI-PIECE BACKGROUND TECHNIQUES. For a background depicting sky, mountain, plain, lake, or a combination of settings which add locale to your cutouts, you should follow marquetry methods.

Figure 48. Edges produced by a single cut with the saw must fit perfectly, even if your saw wavered slightly because of grain. A minor protrusion on one edge fits a matching indentation in the other edge. Pull edges together and apply gummed tape. Example is Brazilian rosewood.

Figure 49. Knife-cut along guideline to make perfect-fitting joint between sky and mountain.

There are two simplified ways: saw-cutting as explained in Chapter 8 and knife-cutting.

KNIFE-CUTTING TEMPLATE METHOD.
In this example, we are using pale gold avodire for the sky. Cut a sheet oversize at all edges. Tape the avodire to your workboard. Using your full-size pattern, trace the sky/mountain line on the avodire. Cut along the guideline with your craft knife and remove the bottom waste piece. Leave the sky taped to the workboard at sides and top. Prepare an oversized sheet of Brazilian rosewood for the mountain. Slip the rosewood about ½" under the bottom edge of the sky line. Mark a pencil guideline on the rosewood by using the avodire

sky line as a template. Move the rosewood onto your workboard and knife-cut along the guideline (Figure 49). This use of one cut edge as a template for the adjoining edge is one of the simple secrets of successful knife-cutting marquetry. It produces a far better joint than you could get by tracing the sky line twice.

Fit the two cut edges together and use snips of brown gummed tape to hold the rosewood mountain to the avodire sky (Figure 50). Continue the face assembly by starting again with the first step; that is, trace your next full-size pattern line onto rosewood to establish the cutting line along the bottom edge. You need to tape the first two parts together, though, to locate this new cutting line accurately.

Figure 50. Assemble sky and mountain with gummed tape. To complete this marquetry assembly for your mounting panel, proceed in the same way with next piece, starting by tracing pattern along lower edge of rosewood mountain where it will join with open field or lake.

Make the cut and use the bottom cut edge of the rosewood mountain as a template for the third veneer, whatever you have chosen for the open plain or far shore of a lake where it meets the rosewood mountain.

When the face assembly is complete, held together with tape, turn it over, scrape filler into the joints, and lay the glue-fresh mounting panel onto the veneer assembly. Trim all overhang when the glue is dry. In Chapter 15 you will discover how a few extra steps could have turned the assembled veneer face into a complete marquetry picture before it was glued to a panel.

GLUING TECHNIQUES. If you use liquid glue, you have a choice of white or yellow. Both of these glues, presented in Chapter 3, are handled the same way. Squeeze glue around the center of the panel and toward the edges, but not too close to the edges. Spread glue with brush or wooden comb from the center outward across the edges. Be sure to provide even, somewhat full coverage everywhere. Don't slight the edges when brushing. Later you will get some glue squeeze-out around the edges when clamps or weights are applied. If you don't, you know that you haven't provided sufficient coverage.

Veneer one side of a mounting panel at a time, then clamp or weight it with adequate pressure all over. Leave it overnight before trimming the overhang.

The alternate method for making a multi-piece background for a mounting panel uses the saw pad technique. It produces closer-fitting parts and is recommended to anyone owning a 12″ fret saw, which is needed to swing around corners of the pad. Trial assemble the parts on the dry mounting panel and attach them with gummed tape (never clear) and glue assembly to the panel, tape side up.

CLAMPING VENEER PANELS. A system of heavy weights is adequate for pressing glued cutout parts to panels, but clamps are better for face veneering. Face veneers, whether one-piece or an assembly of joined and taped pieces, require uniform, heavy pressure across the center and out across all edges. If this kind of pressure is not provided, the face veneer is apt to blister within the panel and to lift somewhere around the edge. Weights cannot dependably provide the kind of overall pressure needed.

Figure 51. Angle irons from junkyard make best crossbearers for applying adequate clamping pressure across central areas of large panels. Wood crossbearers bow at the middle.

CAULS. When gluing a face veneer to a mounting panel, you need a flakeboard caul on top and one underneath the panel. Ideally, cauls used with clamps should be the same size or ½″ larger at every edge than the panel being clamped. Have enough cauls for two or more simultaneous clamping jobs.

Here is an effective crossbearer—an angle iron from the junkyard (Figure 51). This simple device allows you to use smaller C-clamps than required by equally strong heavy wooden crossbearers. All panel veneering is safer with some form of crossbearer. A panel about 18″ square needs a setup equal to the one illustrated;

smaller panels can get by with somewhat less. Even a 10″ x 12″ panel should have at least four clamps.

Some glue containers suggest thirty minutes' drying time in clamps or under weights, but those instructions don't apply to veneering. The best practice is to leave the work under pressure overnight. If this is not practical, allow at least four hours before removing clamps or weights. Even then, leave a caul on top to reduce penetration of humidity from the air. Do not trim overhang for at least twelve hours.

TRIMMING. Turn the panel over, with veneer side lying flat on a clean, smooth surface where there is no chance of its being scratched when you pivot the panel to trim the overhang. Fit your craft knife with a fresh, sharp blade. When you trim overhang, you may find that some veneers tend to chip at the cut edge. Using a super-sharp blade is the first preventive measure. The next is laying a strip of clear tape on the opposite side of the veneer, along the cutting line. This keeps the veneer cutoff strip from breaking away when only partly cut through. Tape laid on top, over the cutting line, is useless. When the cut is finished, remove tape slowly and gently. Start it with a knife point as necessary, but don't gouge the veneer.

There is a trick to laying tape under the cutting line. First, it is much easier to remove without knife gouges if you leave the end hanging over the veneer edge. This piece gives you a fingerhold. Lay tape in short lengths, not one long strip; short lengths are easier to handle. Next, let each succeeding piece overlap the piece before it. In this way you usually can take hold of one end and peel off the entire strip in one cautious pull. If you peel tape carelessly, it will lift a few fragments of veneer edge with it. Remove clear tape from veneer as soon as it has served its purpose. If left on, it becomes harder to remove.

There is a trick to tape disposal. Used clear tape is still sticky and stubborn. It will stick to your fingers as you peel it from veneer. The quickest way to get rid of it is to deposit each tiny piece on a scrap of newspaper just as soon as you peel it off.

SANDING PANEL EDGES. All trimmed panel edges need sanding. If you finger-sand, you will surely round the edge, so use your sanding block and keep it flat on the edge. Stroke long-grain edges with the block at an angle to prevent sandpaper

edges from picking up a fine sliver and ripping it into a major flaw. Stroke end grain gently away from the face veneer. If you pull the sanding block forward, across end grain, you run the risk—almost a certainty—of chipping.

PRE-SANDING VENEER PARTS. An occasional sheet of veneer will show ridges, caused by manufacturing processes, crate marks, chalk symbols added for identification, ink-stamped numbers, or other unnatural disfigurements. Try erasing these marks with an ink eraser. If that fails, you will need to sand these unwanted blemishes. You can pre-sand veneer sheets more safely before you knife-cut or saw them into delicate parts. Use a sanding block and sand far enough afield of the blemish to blend the color tone.

Sometimes a project requires a perfect edge on a veneer strip that is to be laid flush against another edge. You can perfect the cut edge by stroking the strip across a full sheet of sandpaper. To prevent the sandpaper edge from picking up a sliver, stroke only on the sandpaper, not inward across an edge.

When the edge is end grain and a brittle wood, follow the same sanding method and back up the edge with a scrap of heavier wood (Figure 52).

VENEER EDGING. Mounting panels made of hardboard up to a ¼″ thickness look fairly nice without edging. They can be prefinished in a variety of ways. Black paint gives them a natural-looking shadow and makes them surprisingly inconspicuous. Gold paint is an alternative, but it emphasizes the edge, and this may or may not be desirable.

Wood trim is recommended for edges over ¼″. To apply wood trim, first remove

Figure 52. When sanding end-grain edge to perfect a joint, backing it up with scrap strip can reduce chipping.

the curl by flexing a strip over a rounded table edge, veneer side against the table. Next, spread contact glue on edge and trim. When dry, place a slipsheet of wax paper between the two surfaces, except at the starting end. Align one edge precisely. Withdraw the slipsheet gradually as you finger-press the edging to the panel (Figure 53). Roller the trim hard against the panel. Trim off the overhang and save the overhang strip for a future job.

Figure 53. Apply edging with contact glue. Separate surfaces with slipsheet of wax paper. Align one edge perfectly. Withdraw slipsheet a little at a time, pressing surfaces together.

CHAPTER 10

Applying Cutouts

With all parts cut out and a mounting panel prepared, you are ready to assemble your design. You will learn that saw-cut parts generally fit together better than knife-cut parts, since knife-cutting involves two separate tracing operations and two separate cutting operations which magnify the slightest deviations from the line. Sanding and trimming usually correct these flaws; even the experts have to do it to their work. It is comforting also to remember that craftwork is not intended to be machine stamping. Slight variation at joints can be expected and, indeed, can be regarded as proof that the work was hand-made, a quality to be admired. In the instructions to follow, you will discover ways to minimize imperfections that bother you.

TRIAL ASSEMBLY. Test the cut parts in a dry assembly as soon as the last one is cut. If a design is composed of many parts, you should "trial assemble" it on the original pattern. This practice reveals outline irregularities as well as mistakes that may have occurred anywhere along the line, from making your work patterns into separate pieces to cutting the parts. At this point you can correct some of the workmanship problems by sanding, or you can

remake a part correctly or better. Now is the time to discover mistakes, not after you have glued down several parts.

SANDING CUTOUTS. Some edges of cutouts, both knife-cut and saw-cut, can be improved by careful touch-up sanding. Bottom edges of sawed parts occasionally have a fuzzy burr from sawing. Use the variety of sanding sticks shown in Chapter 3 for this task. With a little practice, you will be able to hold a knife-cut part freehand while you rotate a round sanding stick along its very delicate inside curving edges. Hold the part in one hand with fingers fairly close to the edge being sanded, and with the other hand apply a sanding stick cautiously and with a very light touch (Figure 54).

Stroking along the edge, over and over, is the safest technique. Never do any cross-edge sanding unless an intricate shape leaves no option. In this case, sometimes you can lay the cut part on a small workboard at the edge of a table, with the cut edge hanging over, and hold the part down with your fingers close to the edge while you work a sanding stick with the other hand (Figure 55). You will find your

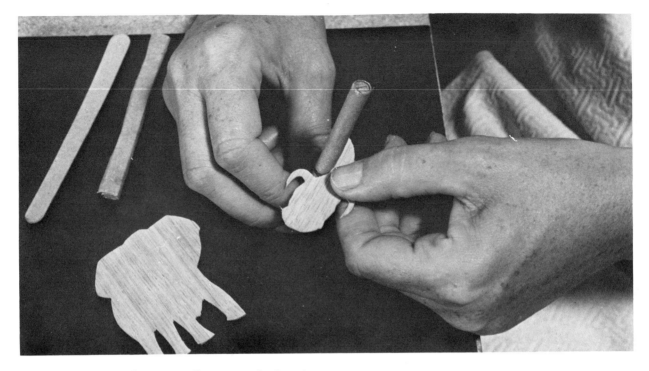

Figure 54. Touch-up sanding on elephant's trunk perfects the outline. Hold fingers close to sanding edge for maximum protection of cutout.

Figure 55. The horse cutout is too fragile for freehand sanding. Hold it down on a workboard at table's edge and sand beyond the edge.

own little tricks for safe sanding as situations occur.

Where you have a sawed form left over, such as a saw pad piece which matches the design part, use it to protect the veneer while sanding. Sandwich veneer back in position in the pad, edges aligned. Tape or squeeze the form together and sand the form as well as the layered veneer. Balsa pads will sand down as fast as the veneer (Figure 56). If any other forms or shaped cauls are left over, use the caul as a sanding form.

Sanding to perfect exterior edges of cutout parts is always good practice, but sanding edges that fit together presents a problem. If you can improve a joint, sanding is advisable, but continually fit dry parts together to see that you haven't opened the joint noticeably. If this happens, you can

Figure 56. When you have a shaped form left over from a saw pad, replace cutout between matching pads and sand edges together. Pad sands as easily and as fast as veneer.

sand the adjoining part to compensate—not always practical—remake the over-sanded part, or press filler into the joint after assembly. If you decide to remake the part, use the second part, that is, the adjoining part, as a template to lay on the new piece of veneer for pencil-tracing an accurate cutting line.

GUIDELINES. After cut parts have been satisfactorily fitted, make a dry assembly on the mounting panel, determining the location that looks well balanced. Select the part you want to put down first, usually the largest part, around which other parts will be arranged. With a very sharp pencil, make short, light guidelines in about three places, as close as you possibly can to the cutout. These lines won't mar your finished product. If they show up at all on light wood, they look like natural shadow lines. On dark wood they disappear.

LAYING OUT PANORAMIC DISPLAYS. The numerous components to be assembled in large pictures, especially "Africa," "Undersea World," and "Prehistoric America," are too precious for extensive handling. It is better, therefore, to make paper cutouts or pattern tracings of the subjects and shift them around on the mounting panel until you determine the location for each piece. Use a snip of masking tape on paper cutouts. It allows easier lifting and shifting than clear tape.

GLUING CUTOUTS. Only two of the glues recommended in Chapter 3 are suitable for mounting cutouts: white glue and yellow glue. Contact glue requires coating both surfaces, and this is not possible for cutout mounting. The slight advantage of white glue is that it sets more slowly, which allows a little more time to slide the part into precise location. The advantage of yellow glue is its stronger holding power, which could make it a better choice for extra-dense, oily woods or woods having a natural tendency to buckle.

The gluing qualities of woods differ, as woods vary in porosity and composition. Macassar ebony is dense and oily; Brazilian rosewood and bubinga are oily. Thus these three woods are a little harder to glue than open-grain species. Fresh glue may pull away from the edges when you are waiting the required three minutes for tack to develop. Inspect the glue coverage every minute and recoat where necessary.

The gluing techniques in Chapters 9 and 12 apply to panel veneering, where you spread glue on the panel or core, not on veneer. That is the right way when you have the option. The reason is simple. White and yellow glue harden by giving up moisture. They give it up very fast. Moisture going into a panel or core is more easily absorbed without damage than moisture going into thin veneer. Moisture makes veneer buckle, and some veneers buckle quite fast. When you are mounting cutout parts, you have no option but to spread glue on veneer, as it would be completely impractical to spread glue on a panel.

To offset the buckle, hold the veneer down with a dull-pointed awl (Figure 57) or with tweezers until the three-minute tacking period is over. Stickiness, or tack, develops when the glue is exposed to air. In about three minutes the glue surface is ready for you to lay the part on the panel.

With most veneers, you can work safely on newspaper when gluing. They will not mark dark woods. Have several stacked

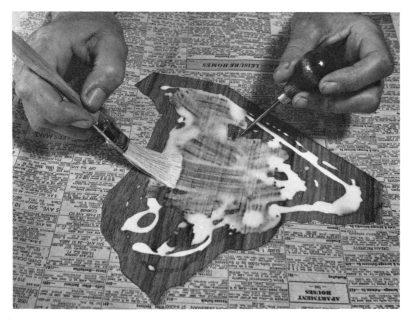

Figure 57. Veneer buckles when it absorbs moisture from fresh glue. Use a dull-pointed awl to reduce buckle and to prevent shifting from the pull of the glue brush.

sheets so that one sheet after another can be removed as it becomes glue-smeared where your brush goes over the edge. Gluing light veneers calls for more caution. With light-colored veneer, gluing on clean white paper or a cut-up brown paper bag is much safer.

Moving glue-fresh parts to the mounting panel with tweezers is best, as tweezers leave no thumb prints in the glue.

When gluing tiny parts to a mounting panel, keep a very small mound of fresh glue on wax paper near you. With an artist's fine brush, you can pick up just a touch of glue from the mound. Hold the tiny part with tweezers, and sometimes between fingers, while applying glue with the brush. Fold the paper over and start a new glue mound as the first mound dries out.

WEIGHTING. Designs composed of many small parts, such as the figures in "Sports," often can be assembled one part right after another. When you assemble in this way, provide your worktable with a heavy iron or brick for temporary weighting as in Figure 58. Lay wax paper over the glued area of the design; place the weight on top. If practical, use a large enough weight so that eventually it can cover the entire assembly.

Temporary weighting should be for a short work period because you sometimes take a slight risk that the glue will not bond correctly. With unruly veneers, however, that show a natural tendency to curl, don't take any chances. It is safer to weight each piece immediately after laying, and leave it for at least an hour before continuing assembly. If working like this, more or less on the hour, is inconvenient, leave the partial assembly under weights for a longer period, not shorter. Poor weighting practices can ruin good cutouts.

With the occasional exception of tempo-

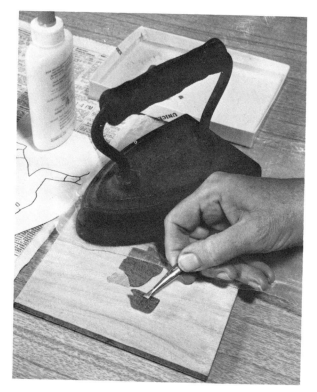

Figure 58. You can assemble tiny parts, one after another, if you cover work in progress with wax paper and heavy weight.

pery. You can minimize squeeze-out somewhat by waiting four minutes for tack to develop. But don't carry this trick too far. And never try to reduce squeeze-out by using lighter glue coverage at the edges.

Next, place your cutout assembly (on mounting panel) onto the wax or brown paper and cover with a second sheet of either one. Position top caul; clamp and weight. If the cutout is built up and has more than one plane, have about six small sheets of newspaper ready to lay as a cushion over the wax paper or brown paper which covers the veneer.

When you are assembling designs of more than one plane, complete all first-plane parts before laying parts on the second plane, and complete the second plane before starting the third plane.

rary weighting, follow the rule that all glued-up assemblies must be weighted heavily, or clamped, just as soon as cutouts are laid on a panel. Weighting is generally practiced for cutout assemblies because it is easier than clamping and requires less investment, often none if you have old bricks on hand. Also, weights can provide concentrated pressure exactly where it is needed.

Prepare ahead of time for weighting. Have wax paper cut just slightly larger than the mounting panel. It is best to put down wax paper where you expect glue squeeze-out to overrun the work and spread to the paper. Where no appreciable squeeze-out onto the paper is anticipated, a single sheet of brown paper bag without seams is preferred because it is less slip-

Figure 59. This is a freshly laid weighted assembly. It consists of a flakeboard bottom caul, a layer of paper, mounting panel and cutout, layer of paper, flakeboard top caul, and bricks for pressure.

Be ready with cauls. If you are using weights, the caul for underneath can be any size larger than the panel. The top one ideally should be the size of the panel or just slightly larger.

In review, the order of layering is this: bottom caul, brown or wax paper, glued assembly on mounting panel, brown or wax paper, newspaper if more than one plane in cutout, top caul, weights (Figure 59).

The problem to watch for when weighting a fresh assembly is shifting of cutout parts. Waiting three minutes or longer before laying a part on a panel, while glue develops tack, reduces shifting, but it does not entirely prevent it. If you think a caul or a piece of the cutout moved as you weighted the top caul, open up the setup for another inspection and readjust the glued part while there is still time.

CLAMPING CUTOUTS. When designs are composed of large cutout parts, or you know the veneer is somewhat unruly and tends to curl, use clamps instead of weights. The same ingredients go into the setup as called for above. However, clamps apply heavier pressure. To spread pressure from edges to center, use crossbearers (Figure 60). Wooden crossbearers are sufficient for small assemblies. Consider jaw opening of available clamps when preparing crossbearers. For extra-large work, nothing is better than the junkyard angle iron crossbearers shown in Chapter 9.

Figure 60. A partial assembly between cauls gets localized heavy pressure from hardboard crossbearer. For larger assemblies, use heavier crossbearers and more clamps.

CHAPTER 11

Filling Joints, Cleaning, Finishing

Marquetarians use powdered wood filler to improve the appearance of their veneer pictures. They pack a mix of fine sawdust and glue into open joints where parts do not fit perfectly, and they blend it so skillfully that most observers are unaware of the filler. Most veneer cutouts can be improved in the same professional way.

The method is the same for filling joints and for patching cracks that sometimes occur in woods which have a strong tendency to curl, such as the illustrated green poplar burl section of the "Modern Art" tray in Chapter 14.

Finely powdered sawdust of a neutral tan color is sold by wood suppliers. It is a useful product to have on hand. However, the best material for patching cracks or loose joints is homemade matching filler.

If you have kept a scrap box of veneer cutoffs and small leftovers, as you should have, locate a piece of the same wood you are patching. Use your veneer saw as a scraper (Figure 61) and make a mound of sawdust on wax paper. Do not use sandpaper to make sawdust, or the sawdust will be loaded with silica. Nothing is better than a fine-tooth saw, not even a chisel. Scrape the sawdust into a mound. Near it, squeeze out a few bubbles of white glue.

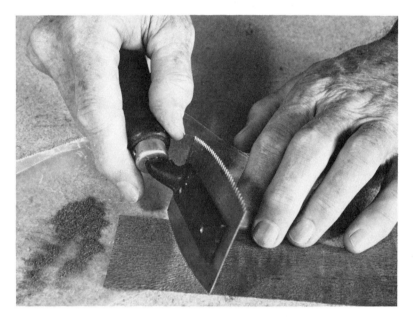

Figure 61. Make your own matching filler by scraping scrap veneer to create a mound of sawdust.

Don't mix them. Make an applicator about ¼" wide from a scrap of veneer. Pick up a small amount of glue on the applicator, then pick up some sawdust from the edge of the mound. All mixing is done with the applicator. If you start by mixing glue into sawdust, the mix will harden before you can use it. For the first application, you want more glue than sawdust on the appli-

Figure 62. Scrape applicator across crack to pack filler mix deep into opening. Example is poplar burl.

Figure 63. Wait several hours or even overnight to scrape dried filler mix from repaired crack or panel joint as shown on pieced benin face veneer.

cator, which will force the glue down into the crack when you scrape the applicator across the crack (Figure 62). Now do the same thing again, except pick up very little glue and plenty of sawdust. This trick forces the matching sawdust into the top of the crack. Let it mound up. Some glue smearing is inevitable, but it will scrape off later. Leave the crack mounded instead of trying to smooth it down. Set the work aside to allow the glue to harden. After two or three hours, try scraping the crack. If you waited long enough, the glue will come loose as a dry powder (Figure 63). If the patch is still gummy, wait longer. Actually, the best practice is to wait overnight before scraping. Follow scraping with gentle finger sanding. If you use a sanding block, you will lighten the area and will then have to sand a larger area to match.

When you have backed a mounting panel with two pieces of veneer, neither of which was wide enough to cover the panel, you will have an open joint. This crack should be filled, not so much for appearance, but to keep out moisture. For such work, the ready-made sawdust filler saves time.

This is a good time to inspect the edges of all parts of the design. Occasionally you will find a loose edge. For this type of repair, white glue is the most cooperative. It flows from the tip of a spatula or knife into the opening as you gently slide the tool under the open edge. Hold the panel in a vertical position to let gravity help move the glue deep into the slit. Wait about five minutes before finger-pressing the part into position. Pick up squeeze-out with a clean knife point. Cover with wax paper and apply concentrated heavy pressure for several hours or overnight.

Again inspect the design around all edges for hardened glue bubbles. Glue bubbles are not hard to remove. Actually they come off a little more easily after the glue has set for only one hour, but after only one hour's drying time be careful not to lift a cutout; the glue underneath has not fully hardened. The chisel blade in your craft knife is the best tool for removing these bubbles (Figure 64). Loosen them carefully from above, coming straight down with the chisel riding against the edge of the cutout. Twist the chisel left and right. After that, get underneath the partially loosened bubble and lift it. Be extra careful with the chisel. Use the wood-carver's technique of braking its forward thrust by restraining it with your free hand as you push the tool forward. This precaution prevents a damaging slip of the chisel.

SANDING ASSEMBLED CUTOUTS. If you applied paper tape to mend a split on any piece of veneer used as part of a cutout, you now must remove the tape. Lightly moisten the tape and peel it off, following instructions in Chapter 13. You should now decide whether to face-sand the assembly. Many craftsmen skip face-sanding because it reduces the interesting texture of wood, and texture accentuates design. If you face-sand a lacewood bird, for instance, the bird loses a lot of the figure, which resembles feathers. And to face-sand the fascinating swirl figure of myrtle which was selected as the sky for "Bighorn I" would erase most of its suggestion of rugged terrain. Face-sanding, therefore, is not recommended as standard procedure for cutouts, but only as a means of cleaning up imperfections or marks acquired in processing, which cannot be removed by a

Figure 64. Use chisel blade to loosen hardened glue squeeze-out around edges of applied cutouts.

typewriter eraser. When sanding is essential, wrap a used piece of your finest sandpaper around a block and stroke gently, taking extreme care not to move the edge of the sandpaper across the edge of a cutout, because that could start a sliver.

BRUSHING. Always after sanding a cutout use a small, clean scrub brush to remove sanding dust and grit from wood pores. Nothing does this job so well as a stiff-bristled brush. Do not rub over a picture with a cloth of any kind. A cloth would surely catch on sharp edges of veneer and cause damage.

TOUCH UP. Ordinarily the natural colors of the veneers you selected should be retained without any applied color. It is easier to achieve strong contrasts in your pictures when you stain various veneers, but this practice undermines the satisfaction that comes from creating design and mood largely with natural veneers.

There are times when stain is an asset, however. A long piece of Brazilian rosewood, for instance, was an ideal choice for the tabletop in "The Last Supper." It is deep brown with characteristic splashes of orange, and it has a restrained and reasonably straight figuration. However, one area was so light that it looked bleached. A mixture of burnt umber and turpentine applied with a cloth blended the light area into the rest of the sheet.

Applying stain to veneer, either before or after the veneer has been glued to its mounting panel, can create a new problem. The veneer will warp in the area where moisture soaks into the wood. After applying stain, either on a loose piece of veneer or on one already glued down, you must weight the veneer heavily until you are ready to use it. If a blister should appear later, follow corrective methods outlined in Chapter 13.

FINISHING. Some professionals use no finish at all on veneer cutouts. If you prefer a finish, apply it sparingly. Furniture may need numerous coats to resist wear, but cutouts are not subjected to wear.

The only suitable finish for veneer cutouts is a low-luster clear finish, such as polyurethane varnish. One of the trade names for this product is Wood-glo. Another trade name for a satisfactory low-luster lacquer is Deft. High-luster material shouldn't be used, as the resulting shine reduces the textural character of veneer because it reflects so much light.

Avoid brush finishing. Edges of cutouts scrape finish from a brush and pile it up. There is nothing you can do to remove this pileup. Finish cutouts by spraying on sev-

Figure 65. Low-luster varnish in spray unit provides best finish for applied cutouts. Never brush-finish cutouts.

eral very light coats of clear finish. Buy an aerosol can of low-luster varnish, or use a small pressure can of the type illustrated (Figure 65). The aerosol pressure can fits on a glass jar. Pour varnish into the jar, attach the pressure can, and spray. If you are not accustomed to spray finishing, the following instructions should be helpful.

Stand the picture plaque upright. Hold the spray unit beyond one end and about 10″ away, in spite of instructions on a can to spray from 6″ to 8″ away. The greater distance keeps the varnish from collecting on the edges. Starting beyond the plaque, come across the upper part of the plaque at an even, moderate speed. Press the spray button fully, not halfway, or the aerosol will sputter and cause a bubbly finish. Do not arc the spray. Move straight across. Do not stop until you have passed the plaque, and do not back up. Repeat the operation for the middle area and for the lower area. Allow twenty minutes for drying and apply a second coat in exactly the same way. That is all the finish your plaque should have. Additional coats will pile up around edges and you will not be able to clean it up neatly. Never rub down cutouts with steel wool or sandpaper.

When you are through spraying, pour the leftover varnish back into its container immediately. Rinse the jar with paint thinner and actually spray some clean thinner through the unit to clean the nozzle.

HOW TO FRAME YOUR PICTURE.
Veneer edging applied around a mounting panel (Chapter 9) completes the plaque. However, why not think about framing your veneer picture?

Having your pictures framed at a local shop is expensive. Buying strips of prefinished molding at the same shop and taking it home to make your own frame saves a little money. The real money-saver, however, is unfinished architectural molding from the lumberyard. Since it doesn't have a rabbeted edge, this type of molding is better suited to most veneer plaques—it doesn't overlap the edges of the plaque. Picture frame molding is less suitable because it has a rabbeted inside edge which forms a lip that extends over the panel, and some cutout parts may extend right to the edge of the plaque.

Many shapes of architectural molding are available. If you find one that is too wide, ask the saw operator at the lumberyard to rip it for you. Lumberyard crews usually will go out of their way to accommodate amateur woodworkers. The two styles of molding illustrated here cost between 10¢ and 15¢ a foot. Both styles were selected for their simplicity. The style mi-

tered and fitted around "Prehistoric America" (Figure 66) is called ogee stop. It is commonly used around window sash. The style for "Africa" (Figure 67) is called shoe molding. It is used as baseboard molding.

Cutting neat miter joints is tricky unless you have access to a miter box. There is no easy, accurate way to improvise. The safest course, even with a miter box, is to cut miters a tiny fraction long and then trim with a handy tool known as a trimming plane. Filing is rarely successful, as a file rounds the miter. With the plane, trim a little at a time and constantly trial-fit to the joining member of the frame.

Figure 66. Lumberyard molding without rabbeted edge is cheapest and best suited to most veneer craft plaques. Cut and fit to panel, then finish before applying to panel.

Figure 67. Strip of mitered shoe molding is purposely wider than thickness of door panel being framed. When applied flush at bottom edge, it rises slightly above panel to form shadow line.

NAMEPLATES. Titles add to many pictures, especially story-telling designs, but any nameplate must be unobtrusive and not conflict with the design. One of the best choices is the embossed plastic label which many stationery stores will make while you wait. Or you may buy a pistol-grip embosser and make your own labels. The most suitable label tape is ⅜″ wide.

Many woodworkers prefer gold tape and place their titles in the center of the lower edge of the frame.

Varnish will give some protection against heat, direct sunlight, and humidity changes, but veneer cutouts can crack even though glued to a mounting panel. To minimize this danger, display your cutouts away from radiator heat and strong sunlight.

CHAPTER 12

Advanced Veneering Techniques Simplified

Without adding to your workshop equipment, you can expand the scope of your work with veneers with a few additional techniques, simplified here for beginners. The techniques include mitering veneer borders for your cutouts and inlaying attractive insets to decorate small gift boxes and other craftwork projects. A short pictorial course in general veneering procedure for beginners and the innovative core principle for making veneered objects that before were not practical are also presented.

MITERING BORDERS. Portrait plaques nearly always look better when bordered. (See "Madonna" in Chapter 14.) Veneer is cut into strips usually 1″ wide for a panel measuring 8″ x 10″ or larger. Strips are joined at the corners in a miter joint. Cut a good miter by following the system illustrated.

Cut four border strips from a sheet of veneer which contrasts but does not clash with either the background or the design. For "Madonna," a 1″ border of gray harewood was planned, and the strips were

cut 1¼″ wide to allow the outer edges to overhang. They were also cut longer than necessary to allow for overhang.

Turn over the mounting panel and

Figure 68. Bordering a picture. Draw pencil layout on back of mounting panel. Extended diagonal is key to this mitering technique.

make your miter layout on the back where pencil guidelines will not be seen when the plaque is hung on a wall. Draw the guidelines 1″ from the edge. Now draw a diagonal from the corner of the panel through the point where the guidelines cross, extending the diagonal as shown (Figure 68). This extended diagonal is the key to the system.

To cut the miter, tape two border strips of harewood in position, overlapping at the ends and overhanging the panel at edges and ends (Figure 69). While holding your straightedge firmly along the diagonal, use your craft knife to cut through the overlapping strips. Don't let the straightedge move until you have finished cutting through both pieces. You now have a good

Figure 69. To cut an accurate miter, tape two border strips on guidelines on back of panel. Extend diagonal line across the overlapping strips. Cut through both strips, using straightedge for guide.

joint. Mark the strips as a pair to be glued together at the face side corner. The side you mark for identification will be glued down. If your miter joints need filling, use methods detailed in Chapter 11.

INLAYING. One of the highly prized skills in veneering is inlaying. The method used by artisans from Egyptian to modern times is too involved for the scope of this book and too difficult for a newcomer, so a simplified technique will be demonstrated. The project chosen for inlaying is the box being veneered in Chapter 14.

One of numerous styles of veneer-face insets, a sunburst design, was bought ready-made. It comes factory-assembled with gummed paper on what will become the face side. The box lid is being veneered with a sheet of mahogany pommelle. The trick to this inlay procedure is cutting an oval in the veneer before gluing it to the lid.

Draw centerlines on the tape side of the inset and on the underside of the mahogany face. Lay the inset in position and trace a pencil line around it. Use your craft knife to cut the oval opening (Figure 70). Cut just inside the pencil guideline and use round sanding sticks to refine the opening to the exact size. This piece is now ready for gluing to the box lid. The alternate method for cutting the oval opening is the saw pad method. With this method, the starting hole for the saw blade is drilled within the oval, and the mahogany oval becomes waste. The saw pad produces an identical mahogany face with oval opening, ready for gluing to the box lid. Glue down the face, allow it to dry, and trim overhang from the four edges before inlaying the sunburst inset. Trial-fit and sand the inset where necessary to perfect the joint.

Now the lid is ready for inlaying. Glue

Figure 70. Use your craft knife to cut an oval opening in the mahogany veneer face.

Figure 71. Veneer face was glued and trimmed before inset was glued in place. Stubborn paper tape is now removed by patient light sponging and scraping.

the sunburst inset, paper side up, in the recessed oval. Apply weight or C-clamps overnight. Next, remove paper tape by moistening and scraping (Figure 71). Be patient. This takes time. Soaking the paper for quick removal will end in disaster. The trick is to apply no more moisture than is absolutely essential. Moisten the tape, wait a few moments for the glue to soften, then peel the tape. Use a thin spatula or a chisel blade to start the stubborn tape. Moisten again lightly and peel anything that sticks up. Do not sand. If you try to hurry removal by over-wetting, the delicate veneer parts will curl, loosen, and possibly lift out with the tape. Moisten lightly, peel, and scrape. There is no better way. Stop the work after most of the tape has been removed, even though some tape and

gummy residue remain. Lay brown paper on top to absorb moisture. Cover with a caul and heavy weights. Leave the project for a couple of days. When dried out, the tape and residue will scrape off with a chisel. Pack wood filler and white glue into the joint. After that, you can sand the inlay for final cleanup.

This time-consuming and uninspiring task of removing tape applies only to ready-made veneer assemblies, including large checkerboard faces taped together. Strips of tape which you apply to join two pieces of veneer or to mend a split will come off easily when moistened once.

Insets like the sunburst present the veneer craftsman with an easy means of adding decorative themes to his craftwork. They are available, ready-made, in an extensive variety of designs, including floral patterns, wildlife motifs, American spread eagle, and single monogram initials. Sizes range from approximately 2″ to 8″ in diameter or width. All insets are ¹/₂₈″ wood assemblies held together by a thick crisscross of brown paper tape.

Instead of gluing down the veneer face and then fitting and gluing the inset in place, you could elect to assemble face and inset with tape, then fill the joint from underneath and glue the one-piece assembly to the lid. This system is best for improving a poor joint.

GENERAL VENEERING PROCEDURE. Cutting and mounting veneer shapes to create

decorative plaques is one of the fun ways to use veneer. Inlaying, as presented above in its simplest form, is an easy way to add decorative motifs to veneered surfaces.

There is another broad area open to anyone who likes to work with veneer; let's call it general veneering procedure. It involves the basic techniques of applying veneer to almost any smooth, flat wood surface regardless of size. Even the simplest application of skills you learn in this general veneering procedure can be rewarding. The example given here is a gift set of coasters (Figure 72). When you wish to apply the same skills to larger projects, you will be able to cover scarred tabletops with beautiful new veneer and to enrich

Figure 72. Both coasters are faced with eucalyptus veneer. To demonstrate general veneering procedure, a useful skill to acquire, one was accomplished with white glue, the other with instant-setting contact glue.

cabinet doors, chests of drawers, head-boards, and other plain surfaces.

In Chapter 9, you discovered ways to veneer mounting panels. This chapter duplicates a few of the steps learned, but also covers more and should provide a quick understanding of the basic techniques of general veneering procedure.

It is useful to learn two practical gluing methods. White glue is ideal for most craftwork and is entirely satisfactory for veneering a set of coasters. However, other veneering projects involving sheets over 12″ square are easier when you can use contact glue. Both gluing methods are shown.

Contact gluing method starts with same pencil layout as Figure 73. However, the procedure then changes. In Figure 75, straightedge and knife procedure for contact method leave overhang on only two adjacent edges. Trim top and left edge on pencil lines. Trim other two edges with overhang allowance.

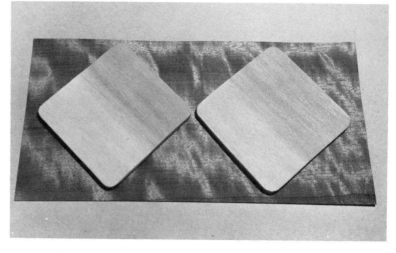

Figure 74. For balanced, nonwarping construction, when one side of core is veneered, the other side also must be veneered. African cherry was chosen for second side, making coasters reversible.

Figure 73. To begin, lay two cores 4″ square, corners rounded with file, on gluing side of 6″ x 12″ sheet of eucalyptus veneer. Stable, nonwarping cores were made by gluing together two ⅛″ pieces of poplar with the grain at right angles. Coasters laid at diagonal for interesting figuration. Mark pencil line around cores.

Figure 75. Move straightedge ¼″ outside pencil line to provide overhang. Cut veneer with craft knife.

Figure 76. Squeeze white glue on center of core. Spread out across edges with brush. A fairly heavy coat is best. While waiting three minutes for glue to develop tack, inspect edges. Touch up spots not fully covered. Where you have a choice, always spread glue on core or panel, not on veneer.

Figure 78. Roller hard to assure overall contact of veneer against core. Roller edges with special care to avoid breaking overhanging veneer. Place assembly between flakeboard cauls. Layer with wax paper so that any glue squeeze-out cannot spread onto cauls. Cover with heavy weights, preferably overnight.

Figure 77. After three minutes, lay glue-fresh core on veneer. Pencil marks now guide alignment and leave overhang at all edges.

Figure 79. Lay assembly on clean, smooth workboard, veneer face down. Trim overhang with craft knife. Repeat entire gluing procedure to cover other side of core with African cherry veneer. Sand edges gently.

CORE PRINCIPLE. Veneering two sides of a stable panel to make coasters is an example of practical veneering. Earlier, in Chapter 9, this core principle was used to prepare mounting panels for cutouts. There are other applications of the core principle in this book. In fact, it is one of the most important and useful techniques in veneer craft.

The core principle enables you to make shaped objects. Veneer is too thin and fragile to be handled and used by itself. However, when veneer is backed by a stable core, you can shape it into objects by using a fret saw. The veneered core is sandwiched in a saw pad. You transfer the pattern to the top member of the pad and carry out the work just as for sawing veneer cutouts.

By combining the techniques you have already learned—the saw pad method and the core principle—you can now make a greater variety of veneer craft projects.

Several woods make good core stock. Poplar and bass of ⅛" thickness are entirely stable when veneered on both sides, and they are easy to cut. Plywood should be avoided. A discarded venetian blind slat of birch was used experimentally, and successfully, for the chimpanzee in the trapeze act (Chapter 14). A blind slat is completely warp-proof but a little hard to cut, and it limits you to design parts no wider than 2". However, you can usually find a blind for only one dollar at a flea market.

A variation of the core method is used for the discs that are cut for the jewelry pendant. Standard ⅛" stock is too thick: when veneered on two sides, it will not fit into the grooved bezel of the pendant. Two sheets of East Indian rosewood are cut 2¼" square for face veneers, front and back of the disc. These squares are glued to a center core of Oriental veneer. The as-

Figure 80. Apply contact glue to veneer and to core. Allow to dry for sixty minutes until piece of brown paper bag will slide across surfaces. Repeat glue application to both surfaces. Allow to dry. Keep parts away from each other. They will stick permanently on contact.

sembly is sandwiched in a saw pad of the same size and cut into a circle. The closed pad system is used here, because the thin veneer assembly is safer when protected top and bottom. The heavier chessmen assembly was rigid enough without a top pad.

The variation of the core assembly method used for the pendant disc is called layering. An extra square of veneer substitutes for standard, heavier core stock. You can make a set of coasters with this method, using 4" squares. For larger projects layering somewhat increases the risk of warp, depending on the veneers you select. The prime rule in layering is to crisscross grain; that is, if the core grain runs north and south, assemble the two faces with grain east and west. This arrangement provides the most stable, warp-free panel.

Figure 81. Lay wax paper as slipsheet over core, leaving small exposed margin at top and left where you cut veneer flush, without overhang. These edges are now to be perfectly aligned. First, align top edge of veneer along exposed top edge of core. See that left edges are in alignment, but not yet touching. Press veneer to core along exposed top edge. Gradually withdraw slipsheet as you continue to press veneer against newly exposed surface of core. Watch left-hand edges, maintaining perfect alignment at every move. Roller hard to assure complete, overall contact just as you did in first demonstration (Figure 78). Be careful not to break two overhanging edges. Place assembly under weights for one hour. Trim overhang from two edges (Figure 79). Sand all edges gently.

Figure 82. Edging is optional. If you prefer, prefinish the core edges before veneering. Gold paint would be appropriate. If preferred, follow contact gluing technique for applying edging as in Chapter 9. Slit 1″ wood edging down the middle, as ½″ width is adequate for the coasters. Apply two coats of contact glue to edge of veneered coaster and to edging. Improvise method for holding and rotating coaster, such as C-clamp held as shown. Scraps of wood protect veneer from clamp jaws. Align one edge of edging. Trim overhang from other edge. Sand carefully. Finish with low-luster varnish.

CHAPTER 13

Correcting Veneering Problems

When you work with veneer you can expect a few problems. The logs from which veneer is cut may have come from trees that were twisted and bent by wind, storm, overcrowded forests, growth to reach sunshine, and other vagaries of nature. A tree that led a hard life is apt to have twisted grain, and this condition in turn could show up as warp in a sheet of veneer. The heritage and natural growth patterns of some trees also contribute to warp. Some veneers nearly always have warp tendencies. Zebrano, bubinga, dyed woods, burls, and crotches usually have warped to some extent by the time you are ready to use them. Veneers of the same species do not always act the same. One piece of African cherry may be perfectly flat, while another piece might be slightly wavy. Of course any veneer will warp under poor storage conditions and from rapid changes in heat and humidity.

WARP. Warp is the most common veneer fault and is about the easiest condition for you to correct. First, you must decide whether to flatten the entire sheet or cut off a portion a little larger than you need and flatten only that portion. If you see that you can cut off a work piece without

splitting the veneer, that is the better procedure. If the sheet is badly warped, you probably will split and chip it when you try to lay a straightedge across it and press hard enough to cut with veneer saw or knife. In this situation it is wiser to flatten the entire sheet.

Moisten both sides of the veneer very lightly. Dip a whisk broom in a pan of water, flick off some of the water, then flick drops of water onto the veneer (Figure 83). Use a paper towel to wipe the veneer, distributing the moisture. Place the moistened veneer between two flakeboard cauls with brown paper above and below the veneer. Weight the top caul gradually, depending on how badly the veneer is warped. Sudden, heavy weighting will split the veneer. Lay one or two bricks to start. Add more bricks gradually, an hour or more apart. After twenty-four hours, if the veneer is not yet flat enough to use, repeat the entire procedure. If it is acceptably flat, do not moisten again. Change to fresh, dry brown paper, weight heavily, and leave for another twenty-four hours to dry. It is most important that you not glue down damp veneer. Be sure it is completely dry. Veneer flattened in the prescribed manner will not necessarily be tabletop flat. It does

Figure 83. Some veneers have a tendency to warp, such as the poplar burl square shown. To flatten this piece before sawing or knife-cutting, flick water from whisk broom to veneer and place veneer under heavy weights overnight.

not have to be perfect to be workable. When you glue it to a mounting panel, whatever waviness it has retained will disappear.

This flattening process is not permanent unless you now glue the corrected sheet to a mounting panel. Loose sheets will again warp if you put them back with your veneer supply. For this reason, remove the weights from the veneer only when you are ready to work with it. If you set any portion of it aside, weight it again heavily, even if only while taking a walk to the kitchen for coffee.

SPLITS. Severe changes in humidity cause some kinds of veneer to split. As veneer dries out after a period of high humidity or when subjected to home heat, it is apt to split the long way of the grain. Handling in transit from supplier to your home, exposing it to sunshine even briefly, pawing through sheets in your storage boxes, and so on cause brittle veneer to split. Here is a fairly simple remedy for repairing most splits so that they will not be noticed:

Gummed paper of 1″ in width from the stationery store is all you need. Pull the split parts together tightly. Do not let the edges overlap. Lay moistened tape over the split to hold the veneer in place (Figure 84). Press it down hard for several minutes; otherwise it will lift off. Turn the sheet over. Flex open the split very slightly. Run a thin stream of white glue into the open split, and scrape it across. Wipe off the surplus; any remaining glue smear will never be seen because this is the side to be glued down. The taped side is the face.

After you have glued mended veneer to a panel and the glue has thoroughly dried, slightly moisten the tape with a clean sponge, one that has never been used with soap or abrasives. Peel off the tape. If the joint needs filling, follow instructions in Chapter 11. Some of the glue you forced into the split from the back may have squeezed out here. Clean it off with a chisel blade.

AVOIDING PROBLEMS. Thoughtful storage and careful handling can avoid some of the curling and splitting difficulties with veneer. Keep your veneer supply flat at all times, preferably weighted. Standard 4″ x 9″ sheets come from suppliers in boxes suitable for storage. Put partial sheets left from a project in the same box, but keep odd-shaped leftovers and narrow

Figure 84. Split veneer is easily mended. Lay moistened tape over split and roller it hard to assure adhesion. You can work this sheet of taped African cherry without difficulty. Glue down sheet with taped side up.

strips in another box. This practice saves a lot of searching. Leave the boxes in the room where you work unless it is unduly hot or sunny. Never store veneer boxes in sunlight. A cool, damp basement is preferable to a hot furnace room.

Lay workboards or cauls on veneers in process. Put a brick on top even though the piece is being set aside for only a few minutes. After a veneered mounting panel comes out of clamps, store it in the same way, workboard and weight on top, until

you are ready to apply cutout designs. Although most veneers are not so unruly as these work habits may indicate, it pays to protect valuable veneer every step of the way.

Some problems are rarely encountered, but when they do occur, they can be damaging. If you are not forewarned, the knurled collar of your craft knife might scratch a veneered surface. For example, when you trim the overhang of a veneered box, your knife must be close to the adjoining surface. To avoid scratches on the veneer, apply a strip of clear tape where the collar endangers veneer.

Gluing defects: Most problems that show up in completed work could have been prevented. These problems are more apt to occur in mounting panels which you have veneered, rather than in overlaid cutouts, as it is harder to get good glue coverage on larger sheets. The chief cause is poor gluing procedure, specifically, inadequate rollering. Applying hard pressure on freshly glued veneer is the only way to assure firm overall contact. And of course glue coverage must be adequate and overall.

Blisters: Insufficient rollering can easily cause a veneer blister. To flatten a blister, try hard rollering and reclamping. If the blister persists, lay a sheet of aluminum foil over the area. Heat an electric iron to moderate, not high, heat, and iron the blister.

Remove foil; roller the area hard. Repeat ironing and rollering. The hot iron melts the glue underneath long enough to roller it down again. If this second treatment fails, the glue coverage under the blister is inadequate. Slit the blister at two sides and force white glue through the slits. Use finger pressure on the blister to distribute the glue. Roller it hard and apply clamps or heavy weights.

Edge lifting: If a veneer edge lifts from its panel, you either failed to provide adequate glue coverage at the edge or did not clamp or weight the edge uniformly. To repair a lifted edge, prop and support the panel upright. Open the slit gently with a thin spatula and squeeze a few drops of white glue into the slit. Cover the area with wax paper and a heavy wood block. Protect the opposite side of the panel with a scrap of wood. Apply a C-clamp and leave it for twelve hours.

CHAPTER 14

Veneer Craft Projects

The fun of veneer craft is putting your hands to work. You have learned most of the basic techniques from the instructions and photographs—now pick a project that can put your knowledge into practice. Think about which plaque you would like to own or to make as a gift and consider the tools and materials you own and those you will have to buy. Of course, the project you like most might be one of the hardest for a newcomer to make, so consider one of the easiest projects in the book, the key finder. The sports figures are also a good

choice, not because they are so easy, but because they provide the best practice in knife-cutting using the smallest amount of material, and knife-cutting is the most important technique to develop in veneer craft.

As you progress, you will want to make more and more of your own designs. Even then, you can make good use of the designs in this chapter. You can lift an animal pattern, a tree or shrub, sky and mountain, horse, flower, frog, or fish and build your own setting around any of these patterns.

SPORTS GALLERY

Eight popular and exciting sports are represented in this collection of action figures. Only four designs are illustrated here; however, those four show the procedure you follow to develop the entire gallery of eight, patterns for which are included here.

In order to encourage everyone interested in sports to make some of these cutouts, I chose the knife-cutting technique. All you need is a craft knife and a small selection of veneers. To keep this project easy, select a pack of 6″ x 12″ sheets of 1/40″ veneer, since it is the easiest to knife-cut.

If you cut the necessary parts from concentrated areas of the sheets, you will have enough veneer left to provide eight sheets of 5¾″ x 7″, the amount you need for faces and backs of four mounting panels. One standard pack, used economically, provides you with all the veneer you need to make four sports figures and four attractively veneered mounting panels.

Mounting panels for the figures should be 5¾″ x 7″ squares of hardboard or flakeboard. Veneering the panels is optional, but it does give a finished appearance. Whenever you veneer the face of a panel, you must also veneer the back to prevent warp.

A 6-foot length of molding from the lumberyard is more than enough for two gallery strips to display your four sports figures on the wall.

FITTING. Nearly all parts composing the sports figures are curved. Many are small and delicate. Some of the knife-cut edges may need improvement by gentle sanding. Go through a trial assembly of dry parts, as

Trace pattern parts to veneer in compact areas to make maximum use of sheet. Cut outlines with craft knife.

this example of the baseball player shows, to see where sanding should be undertaken with safety.

ASSEMBLING AND GLUING. As always when assembling designs with multiple parts, lay a few large parts, dry, on the panel and mark guidelines. Here, the torso is the best part to put down first. Use white glue. Weight the assembled part for at least five minutes before repeating the operation quickly for the next key part, the legs. Some parts of the sports figures are tiny and have very little gluing surface. Allow extra time under weights as you proceed with gluing. Do not hurry through the assembly.

"BIRDS IN FLIGHT"

Three birds of different sizes are at different angles, climbing and diving above the ocean. This device of depicting different sizes of the same subject establishes perspective.

For striking contrast, I selected white bird's-eye maple for all three birds. If they had been made of different colors of veneer, the illusion of perspective would be lost, because then the birds would be seen as different species in a single vertical plane.

The birds for this panel were saw-cut, but you can knife-cut them, if you observe the rules for cutting points such as beaks and wing tips. In fact, this design is an appropriate choice for one of your earliest knife-cutting projects.

A two-piece background of avodire for the sky and Gulf-Stream green for the ocean was made by cutting and fitting two pieces along a line representing cresting waves. The finished plaque is one of the gallery pictures at the beginning of Chapter 1.

This bird design is also an excellent subject for simplified marquetry. Follow the technique demonstrated for "Bighorn II" in Chapter 15. Keep the project simple by using a one-piece veneer background. Start with a mounting panel about 8″ x 12″ and veneer the back with poplar or sycamore for balanced construction. For the face veneer, use an oversize sheet of chinawood which perfectly depicts a sunset sky. Suggested title for this marquetry plaque: "Pacific Sunset."

"WHITE ROSES"

Most people who have seen this plaque have not realized what was accomplished here. They assumed it must be very difficult to cut all of those pieces. Actually the project is quite easy. The three roses are identical. Each was tilted just enough in assembly to make it look unique. Furthermore, all three came out of one saw pad. This demonstration provides an ideal example of the value of the multiple saw pad.

One pattern is cut apart so that the parts can be spaced on the top blind to keep the saw pad stable throughout the sawing operation. Three sheets of white bird's-eye maple are layered in the pad.

Stem and leaves are easily knife-cut from dark green veneer. The plaque is veneered with mahogany mottle, grain horizontal.

The technique of building a rose from separated single petals has many applica-

tions. As an example, a second rose with fewer parts was knife-cut, and the parts were mounted on a small plaque veneered with bubinga, and a photo easel was attached to the back for use on desk or dresser. This small rose is also white, but could have been made of pink, red, or yellow veneer. Dyed veneers come in these appropriate colors.

Three white roses are sawed in one pad. Cut pattern apart and cement to top blind of 4″ x 7″ pad far enough apart to maintain stable pad as you cut around petals.

Make your own rose design. Knife-cut petals from white, pink, red, or yellow veneer. Mount with green stem and leaves on easeled plaque for desk or dresser.

"THE LAST SUPPER"

This modern interpretation of the da Vinci painting is an impressive plaque 24" long. All parts are knife-cut, and each disciple is represented by veneer of a different color and grain pattern.

A ready-made mounting panel ¼" x 12" x 24" faced with mahogany is a good choice because it affords a light-toned neutral background for the many contrasting elements of the design. For the long rectangular tabletop in the foreground, cut a 3⅝" x 22" sheet of dark-toned Brazilian rosewood, or similar veneer, and glue it to the mounting panel. Cut the chalice and bread from gray harewood, and apply a long, thin oval of purpleheart to represent wine in the chalice.

All figures in the design are triangles which you can lay out directly on veneer without making a pattern. The figure of

Christ, cut from white bird's-eye maple, is 2¼" at the base and 4½" in height. The halo is a 2½" diameter disc of avodire which is notched to receive the point of the triangle. The face is butternut, chosen thoughtfully so that its grain pattern creates a suggestion of a bearded face.

Disciples are also triangles, some thin, some wide. The triangle for the figure at the far right measures 1⅜" at the base and 2½" in height. Create the angles at which the disciples lean in conversation by cutting the base of the triangles at an angle. The tips of all triangles are cut off very slightly, and the heads, which appear to overlap, actually are notched.

You will observe that only eleven disciples are represented and that a seating place second from right is left empty for Judas.

"UNDERSEA WORLD"

This is the easiest of the three panoramic displays illustrated, because it utilizes the simplest mounting panel. All of the creatures of the deep are overlaid on a ready-made ¼" x 12" x 24" plywood panel faced with a veneer of oak. I chose oak because it makes a neutral background. If the undersea world intrigues you or you live near the seashore where the subject is part of your life, you might expand this idea into a grand panorama several times this size. You might include a sea chest with the traditional pieces of eight spilling out or add more sea creatures, large and small, by referring to instructions for making patterns, Chapter 4.

Although an undersea view can be depicted as a vertical cross section without depth of perspective, the scene benefits somewhat by perspective. To create the feeling of distance, small seashells lie on the floor of the ocean in the foreground, and the creatures are larger near the foreground. The small octopus, presumably farther away, is identical in shape to the larger creature in the foreground. Both are cut from bubinga.

The saw-cutting technique for making cutouts has the advantage of producing multiple cutouts in one operation. It also enables you to cut with less risk of breaking the delicate, extending fins and tails of the fish and especially the fragile arms of the octopus. The knife-cutting technique is slower for most craftsmen, but it is in the end just as effective. Review knife-cutting techniques before you start on this display.

The largest branching seaweed I knife-cut freehand from purpleheart. The tendril seaweed, less discernible but real, was a whimsical, irresistible addition and introduces the possibility of collage creations in other displays.

"PLAYFUL PANDA"

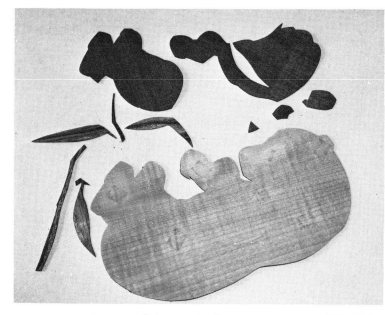

Array of loose knife-cut parts for "Playful Panda" shows how pattern is to be broken up for three kinds of veneer used.

The amusing panda, a natural clown, lies on his back while chewing his favorite candy, bamboo.

The first problem to consider is pattern breakup, and it is solved for you in the photograph of cut parts ready for assembly. The next problem is veneer selection. Pandas are black and white. The license taken in this veneer interpretation makes execution simpler: the body is gray harewood and all other parts of the panda are walnut. Bamboo stem and leaves are paldao. Mounting panel is veneered with curly maple which has the pleasant characteristic of aging from a rather colorless white to soft, pale pink, a factor which greatly accentuates the rippled figuration.

"MADONNA"

Pictorial interpretations of the Madonna have appeared in every painting style. Here a modern interpretation provides a worthy example of how veneers can be used to carry out this timeless theme. The keynote of the design, of course, is simplicity. Almost without detail, this picture is still unmistakably the Madonna.

Color selection plays a vital part in the effectiveness of this plaque. The mounting panel is veneered with purpleheart. The Madonna is made of white bird's-eye maple, and the oval face is bubinga. Radiants are cut from pale gold avodire. Gray harewood border strips, 1″ wide, overlay the panel and confine the viewer's attention to the central design.

"MIDNIGHT RIDE OF PAUL REVERE"

This depiction of the famous patriot and his borrowed chestnut horse roaring through the countryside comes through dramatically with a bare minimum of detail—it is an ideal example of restraint.

Horse and rider are cut of one piece of mahogany or other brown veneer. The church is four pieces with overlaid door, lighted windows, and steeple. There is no separate roadway, no cloud; yet the impression of both is there. The one-piece oak background veneer, which I chose for its converging figuration, creates sky and road while giving movement and direction to horse and mount. A plain background would not have unified the three elements of the design.

Background veneer is always important, but not usually as critical as it is here. Busier designs than this one appear to best advantage with plainer backgrounds.

"TWO FISHERMEN"

Here are two pictures of the ice fisherman's homecoming. In one scene, a seal perched on a rock is observing the occasion. In the second scene, a penguin has taken the seal's place on the rock. This is a case of what's wrong with one of the pictures? Answer: it's the ever-popular penguin. He belongs at the South Pole, not at the North Pole, the land of polar bears. But you can take your choice of patterns.

The featured veneers seem to express their subjects. Eucalyptus veneer, blistered figure, represents the ice-block igloo. Gray harewood contributes a furlike silkiness to polar bear and fur-wrapped eskimo. I used the same veneer for both intentionally; it adds a subtle affinity of appearance and occupation. White bird's-eye maple makes the ice-covered foreground, and reddish crotch mahogany creates the aurora borealis.

Some parts were knife-cut, some were cut in saw pads.

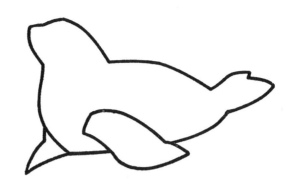

Fishermen plaque in partial assembly. Whether you choose to make penguin or seal as observer, follow technique of making an underlay extended above rock. This method creates a necessary first plane. Separate cutout of penguin or seal becomes second plane overlay.

"DISCOVERY OF AMERICA"

This plaque commemorates the arrival of Columbus in the New World. *Santa Maria, Niña,* and *Pinta* are directing their course toward the tropical island of San Salvador in the foreground.

Consider the background first. East Indian rosewood makes the night sky a deep purple and provides contrast for all elements that stand against it. The moonlit ocean is represented by a fortunate find— finely striped, wavy tamo. The sandy beach of the foreground island is mildly striped Oriental wood. Ships are mahogany with walnut shadows on the water. The moon is avodire. Zebrano makes the ring-marked palm trunks.

If cutting the delicate parts of the ships

is beyond your present level of skill, reduce their detail and make simpler silhouettes.

"MEXICO"

This is an advanced project if you carry it out with all of the fine detail included. However, it is easy to simplify.

You can omit all weaving patterns on the serape over the señor's shoulder and on the poncho worn by the little niño. You can also leave out the blanket on the burro and the leather-strapped sandals on the adults. Horizontal wood grain accounts for the textured dress of the señora, so there is nothing difficult about that. You may be encouraged to try this subject when you learn that all parts except the background were cut with a single-edge razor blade.

Intriguing as the figures and burro may be, they would look less legitimate on a plain background. Quite unobtrusively the background creates a typical Mexican landscape and thus makes a major contribution to the theme. The production technique for this special five-piece interlocked background is detailed in Chapter 8.

"CHARIOT HORSE FRIEZE"

One design of a horse's head is made in three woods and arranged in a modern frieze. The full head, upper left, is African cherry, center is curly maple, right is East Indian rosewood. Cherry is inlaid into maple; maple is then inlaid into rosewood. The entire assembly is a one-plane overlay on a panel of walnut ¼″ x 12″ x 21″. The picture frame is maple.

Either cutting method can be used. The demonstration shows a new adaptation of the saw pad method. One saw pad is used

twice. Layer the pad with three sheets of contrasting veneer, cherry on top. Bear in mind that veneers you select should contrast with each other and with the color of the mounting panel. After cutting the full head outline, open the pad as carefully as possible without shifting the layers. Remove the cherry head and cherry waste.

Close the pad. Before taping it shut, insert three or four pieces of broken saw blades vertically through the outline kerf. They will not go all the way through the

pad if cutouts are out of alignment. Keep working at this procedure until they do go through. You have then fully aligned the components of the pad. Now retape the pad securely.

Next, cut three paper patterns and tape them to the mounting panel in the positions you want the final assembly to have. Trace one overlapping head and neck such as the cherry pattern onto the maple pat-

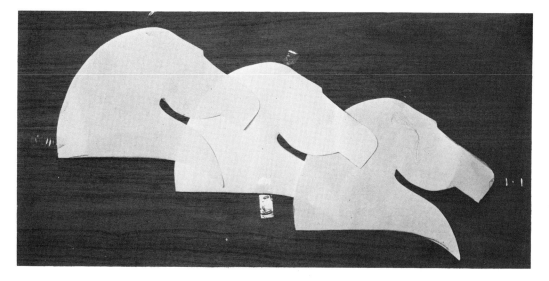

Cut three identical paper patterns of horses. Arrange on 12″ x 21″ panel, overlapping the way you want the final design.

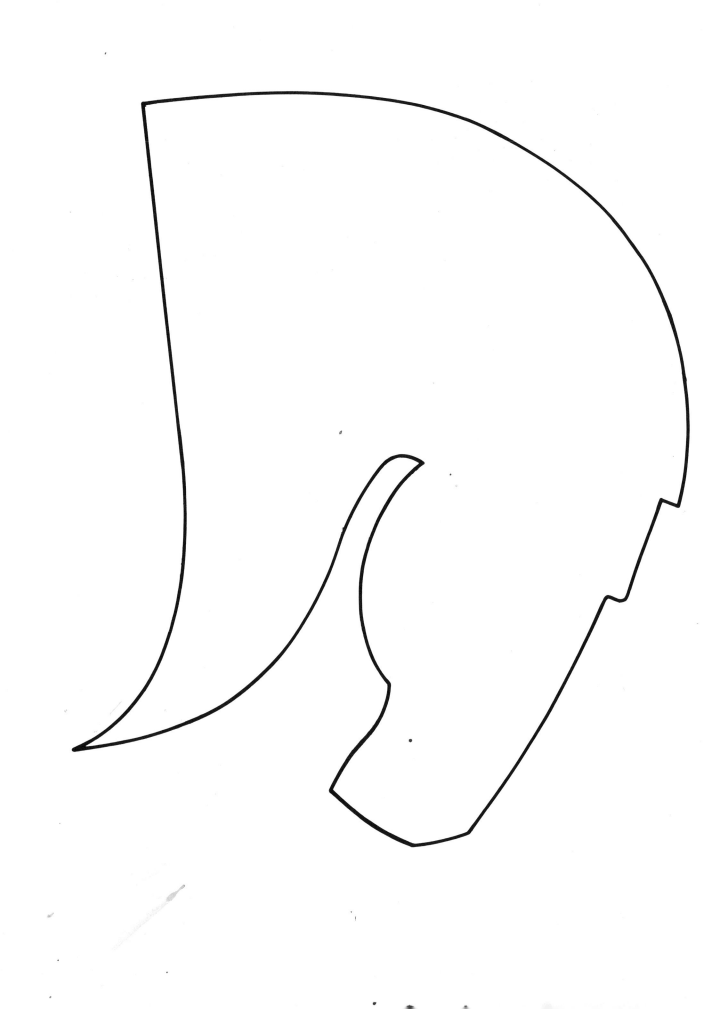

tern. Transfer the maple guidelines to the saw pad. Cut along the newly traced guidelines. Open the pad and you will find the odd-looking maple and rosewood heads ready for a perfect-fitting inlay. One sycamore head was made in the pad as a spare but was not needed. Assemble rosewood on the panel first, then maple, and finally cherry.

After three full heads came from the pad, the inlaying procedure could have been taken over by the template and knife method, similar to the sky/mountain example in Chapter 9. In fact, the entire project could have been accomplished by knife-cutting alone, if preferred.

One cutout head, African cherry, has been removed from saw pad. Pad is closed and sawed again to produce interlock.

"FIRST SWIMMING LESSON"

If you title your pictures, these suggestions may stimulate you into thinking of a storytelling title you like: "First Swimming Lesson"; or "One, Two, Three, Follow Me."

Color selection seems especially important in this design. Selecting three shades of green veneer keeps the design unified, whereas a varied color arrangement could create a spotty, disorganized design. As you examine the illustrations, you will recognize another important factor in color selection, the necessity for contrast between frog and lily pad.

Dyed green veneers are appropriate to the subject and are available in enough different shades to fulfill the requirement for contrast. All four frogs, mama and three little frogs, are made of bright green veneer. All four lily pads are made of dark green veneer, and the dark green is used for foliage at lower right.

The star-shaped flower coming from mama's pad is pink veneer. As you assemble this picture, you will realize how much this single, carefully located pink star helps to direct the eye toward all of the action.

The mounting panel is veneered in pale green veneer sold as Gulf-Stream green.

The saw pad method is demonstrated. Pads I, II, and III for the little frogs contain one sheet of bright green and one

sheet of dark green. This is the mixed pad method. One sawing operation produces two lily pads and two frogs. Since only the bright frog and dark lily pad are wanted, the other combination is filed in a keeping box for a future design.

For mama frog only one sheet of bright green goes into the saw pad. The "no pad" notation means no lily pad veneer in the saw pad. For mama's lily pad and flower, another pad, not illustrated, is assembled with dark green and pink.

While the saw pad method is the easiest way to cut neat, interlocking joints between frog and lily pad, the knife-cutting method can produce all of the parts. The template system for knife-cutting, Chapter 7, is best adapted to this design.

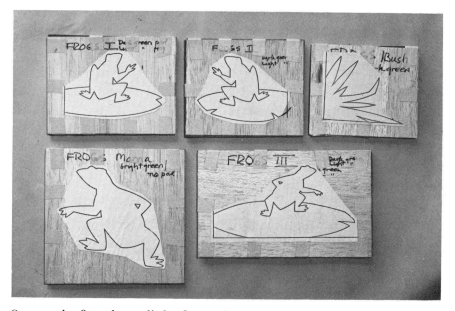

Saw pads for three little frogs demonstrate value of mixed pad method. Each is layered with dark green and light green veneer.

"LION'S PRIDE"

This group of animals seen through openings in African trees introduces another useful design principle. It features the negative shapes of trees, the openings between foliage, branches, and trunks, and is known as negative design.

Negative design gives greater emphasis to the main subject. In this picture, king lion is more dominating than he would be in a more conventional design treatment.

You probably will want to try out the negative design principle some time when you are developing your own theme.

One piece of veneer covers the mounting panel, and the piece you choose must establish the setting. Straight figure will not suggest foliage, but the swirling figuration of walnut butt, used here, suggests in both figure and color what it is intended to represent.

For the saw pad method, the deep-throat fret saw is required. Pay careful attention throughout the sawing operation to be certain that the holes you cut leave trunks and branches connected.

A separate saw pad for the lion is layered with peroba for body and head, Brazilian rosewood for mane. Lioness and peeking cub are peroba.

The entire project can be knife-cut if you do not own a large fret saw.

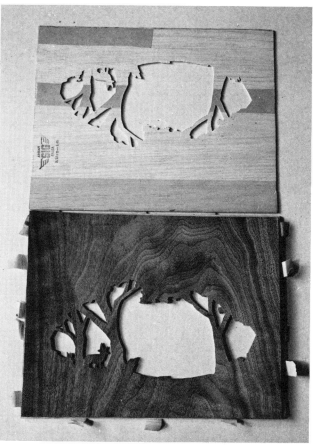

Opened pad reveals square of butt walnut veneer to be applied to mounting panel after negative design has been cut.

"WILD HORSES OF WYOMING"

Aside from creating a nostalgic tribute to one of man's greatest friends in the animal kingdom, this design provides an advanced exercise in veneer craft. It demands good joint making and accurate cutting of delicate parts. If the interlocking horse frieze were set into a background instead of being overlaid, the result would be a complete marquetry picture.

I chose the saw pad method for two reasons: first, it assured the best joints; second, it yielded a large variety of assembly combinations. As a matter of record, parts for twenty-eight acceptable body combinations came from one saw pad. You could go on switching such elements as mane and tail to produce many other combinations. It does not follow, however, that you produce twenty-eight complete assemblies.

If you layer the pad with four sheets of veneer, as this one, you get four complete assemblies. Only the three most acceptable combinations are shown here in loose assembly. The demonstration pad was layered with dark African cherry, used for the lead horse and for mane and tail of the dappled horse. Light African cherry was used for the center horse because I had a sheet with a wavy figure following the body lines of the horse. Olive ash burl yielded the dappled horse, last of the band, and provided the mane for the lead horse. Gonçalo alves provided the black mane and black tail for the center horse.

A grayish green veneer was knife-cut for sagebrush terrain. The plaque was veneered with a sheet of sycamore that had just a trace of pink. To deepen the tone and emphasize the texture of sycamore, I applied natural wood filler and allowed it to dry for several days before gluing the cutout parts to the panel.

Saw pad layered with four veneers produced four complete, mixed assemblies. Only the three best color combinations are shown in loose assembly of parts.

"PREHISTORIC AMERICA"

The animals in this scene once roamed areas of North America where you may now live. They have special names, but generally all are called dinosaurs. The panoramic panel created for the dinosaurs measures 19″ x 31″. The core is hardboard and the backing veneer, laid in three pieces, is sycamore. The frame of ogee stop molding is finished before it is applied.

To achieve a considerable degree of realism the front must be veneered in a combination of colors. Here the sky is represented by sycamore that showed a characteristic tinge of pink. The distant mountain range is gumwood, which is the first veneer to check out when a subject calls for natural-looking mountainous terrain. The entire foreground is Gulf-Stream green, one of the handsomest dyed veneers. I selected a piece that had a few natural dark streaks running diagonally.

Perspective is established here, as in many veneer pictures, by distant sky, then mountains, then broad plain stretching from mountains to foreground. But the mountains will not necessarily appear to be distant unless you follow another design technique. The placement of foreground palm trees in front of the mountains unmistakably pushes the mountains farther away. This is an important principle to remember.

You can achieve the overlaid tree technique only by inlaying the background mountains so that sky, mountains, and plain are in one level plane. Palm trees can then be overlaid on the background.

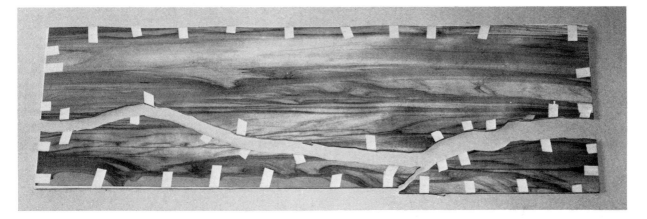

Long pad is cut from both ends and bottom edge to form perfect fit between two mountains and sycamore sky. This is a mixed pad yielding two gumwood mountains at bottom and sycamore sky, beneath gumwood, from upper section.

To inlay the background veneers, you might use knife-cutting methods, but you can do it more easily with a saw pad. Assemble an open pad 33″ long, and layer it with sycamore and gumwood. Cut through from two ends because of limited saw throat.

The bottom edge of gumwood mountains and the top edge of green veneer plain meet in a straight line, unnoticed when trees and two animals partly cover the line.

I used a third device to establish perspective. Notice the two horned creatures in combat in the foreground and the identical creatures, much smaller, far off in the distance at upper right and upper left.

Designs like this which benefit immeasurably from the duplication of animals are accomplished much faster if you use the saw pad method of cutting duplicates in one operation. One of the pair produced in a saw pad can be turned over, as illustrated by the two horned combatants.

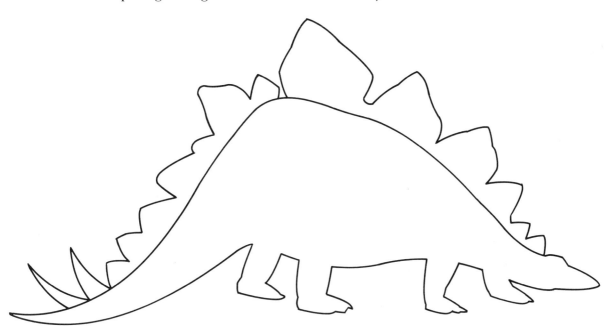

"AFRICA PANORAMA"

The mounting panel for "Africa Panorama" measures 24″ x 38″. Cutting a panel this large is a lot of work; veneering both sides of it means even more work. The problem is easily solved; have your lumber dealer cut down a 24″ hollow core door to the required length. Mounting panel work is simplified further by the use of overlaid mountains.

All lumberyards carry 24″ lauan-faced interior doors. The veneer resembles light mahogany. These panels remain stable forever, they are quite lightweight, and their cost is surprisingly low. Select the door yourself. Avoid blemishes in the veneered face. Be sure to have the panel knife-scored across the face before it is sawed. Instructions for cutting veneered panels without chipping the edges, given in Chapter 9, apply also to sawing this door.

The project breaks down to individual animals. It takes time and patience, but if you have made any of the other projects in this book, you have already acquired all the skills this one calls for. You can cut parts singly with your craft knife or make duplicates in saw pads. Choosing veneer for the animals that inhabit your African plain and arranging them on the panel can be a lot of fun. Part of a rhinoceros coming into the scene at the left and the chimpanzee in the distant tree are examples of whimsical touches.

All of the mountains are overlaid, and you can cut them easily with your craft knife. The largest is gumwood. A smaller Brazilian rosewood mountain, cut on diagonal grain, is overlaid on the gumwood. Mountains are cut apart for two trees. A third tree, the smallest, is overlaid. Be sure

to place a few small animals high on the panel to maintain the illusion of distance.

Shoe molding was applied around the edges to provide an unobtrusive frame and to cover the open end where the panel was cut from the stock door.

"Africa Panorama" is a majestic veneer craft project. Along with "Prehistoric America" it can introduce exciting new decorative displays into your home which will be lasting tributes to your craftwork skill.

PICTURE GALLERY

HOW TO DISPLAY YOUR PICTURES. Two strips of molding attached to a wall provide the simplest display for groups of picture plaques. Single pictures hung with conventional picture hangers are effective and often more desirable because of space limitations or the special appropriateness of a design. However, picture grouping can create an attractive gallery that commands attention.

The easiest way to hold plaques of identical size on the wall is to anchor two strips of molding just the right distance apart to form top and bottom tracks. Plaques are slipped in from one open end and moved

Strips of picture frame molding with rabbeted edge, as cross-section drawing, form top and bottom tracks for your wall gallery.

along until the art gallery is full. One end of the track can start at a corner, but the other end must leave enough space to receive plaques; that is, one end of the track must stop far enough from a right-angled wall for plaques to be inserted. This little detail should be kept in mind when you plan your picture gallery location. The style of molding is shown in cross section.

ARRANGING A GALLERY. Consider the overall artistic impression your gallery will make. Select and arrange your pictures on a table or on a cabinet near a wall before sliding them into the wall track. Try several arrangements. First, try for color harmony with adjacent pictures; second, for tonal contrast, alternating light tones and dark tones; third, for directional design. Where you have a choice, it is better to have pictures at each end pointing toward other pictures rather than pointing outward and taking the viewer's eyes away from the gallery. Always leave at least ½″ between pictures.

SHADOW BOX DISPLAY

Another effective display device, a much more complicated project, is the universal shadow box. It accommodates vertical or horizontal veneer pictures.

This shadow box started with the fifty-cent purchase of a secondhand picture frame. The size of box you build is based on the inside dimensions of the rabbeted frame. Of course, select a frame large enough to receive the plaques you plan to make. Plaques for verticals and horizontals

must be identical in size or they will not be interchangeable in the shadow box.

All cut parts are shown here. Hardboard was used for construction of the box. All hardboard strips except the large back panel were veneered on both sides. Quarter-round molding, painted gold, was used to provide a sliding track, between molding and back panel, for the picture plaque. More molding was cut to go around the outside of veneered sides and

Side panels were veneered inside with prima-vera, outside with mahogany, grain horizontal. Improvised cord clamping arrangement holds box tight while glue dries.

bottom, glued to the back of the frame flush with the rabbet, as a means of adding extra gluing surface to hold the parts in place.

Notice that the top strip of hardboard is narrower than bottom and sides. This arrangement allows the picture plaque to slip into the box from that end, whether the box is hung for verticals or horizontals. The four panels which make up the box frame are glued together. Veneered faces are protected from improvised band clamp by scrap wood strips.

On the back of the large hardboard panel, larger molding was laid to provide more gluing surface for the sides. Blocks were attached, and rings with screw eyes were located equally spaced from the center to hook onto one pair of picture hangers on the wall.

Shadow box parts. Picture frame and quarter-round molding as front stop molding for plaque. Sides and back are same width. Top is narrower to create slot for plaque to enter. Hardboard back panel and molding to hold it in place.

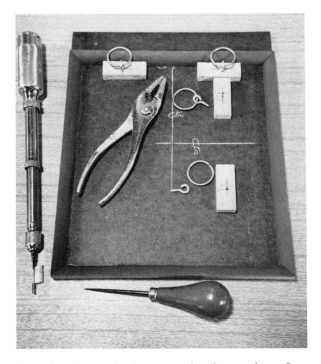

Glue blocks on back to receive brass rings for hanging either horizontally or vertically depending on design of display plaque.

TOAST TONGS

This pair of toast tongs is a beginner's project, useful at the breakfast table, certain to impress breakfast guests, a quickie project, and a desirable gift.

Most drugstores sell tongue depressors, which make excellent core stock for veneering. Buy the 6″ length. You need two for each pair of tongs. Lay them on veneer. Mahogany pommelle 6″ wide was used here. Trace the outlines lightly with a sharp pencil, then lay a straightedge about ⅛″ outside the line to allow margin all around. Cut rectangles with your craft knife.

Spread glue on one core depressor and

Glue mahogany veneer to one side of stick and trim overhang before covering second side.

lay it on the veneer within the outline you traced earlier. Glue the second core to another rectangle of veneer. Layer with wax paper, weight heavily, and leave overnight. The next day, trim the veneer waste by using the core as a guide for your knife.

Next, veneer the other side of the core and trim it. From this demonstration you have learned why it is not practical to veneer two sides of a core at one time: you cannot trim overhang satisfactorily.

Smooth all cut edges by rubbing the assembly across a flat sheet of fine sandpaper.

The two veneered tongs are somewhat stiff and must be splayed. Provide a piece of solid wood ⅜″ thick, ¾″ wide, 1″ long. Taper two faces with a file. Glue the tongs to this spacer block so that they extend about ⅜″ at one end. This setup provides enough spring for toast tongs.

WOMAN'S PURSE KEY FINDER

A tongue depressor from the drugstore is the core for this veneered key finder. Veneer selected was benin. Measuring 6″ long, it is readily located among its mixed companions in an overcrowded handbag.

You veneer the palette in the same way as the toast tongs, then bore a hole for a key chain.

BARN PURSE BOX

The unfinished craft box bought readymade inspired decorative treatment that imitates a hex-painted Pennsylvania Dutch barn.

Start this project by prying off the drive hinges and discarding them. Buy small brass screw hinges for later installation. This operation gets one section of the roof out of the way, making for easier veneering of the box. Mask the outside flat panels of the box; that is, cut cardboard masks to match the two ends and the front and back and tape them in place. Now you can spray the inside of the box and all surfaces of the two roof sections. I used an enamel called Dutch Orange.

When the paint is dry remove the masks. Cut an accurate cardboard template of one end from a manila file folder, the best template material. Trace the template on Brazilian rosewood veneer or on your choice. To me, the figure of rosewood provided the nearest resemblance to weathered wood.

With your craft knife, cut the back edge of the end veneer accurately, without overhang. Cut the front, top, and bottom edges with ¼″ overhang for trimming, but first, to provide a cutting line for these edges, move your template out ¼″ and draw a new guideline.

Glue veneer to one end of the barn at a time. You need heavy blocks of wood, ¾″ preferred, for inside and outside cauls to distribute clamping pressure. The illustration shows the arrangement I used, but you probably could get along with something simpler than a fully shaped outside caul, particularly if you use yellow instead of white glue. Follow the same procedures for the opposite end and then for the front and back. You do not veneer the roof.

HEX SIGNS. Avodire was used for the five quadrant pieces to provide strong contrast with rosewood. Mahogany was chosen for the two stars. Cut the parts with your craft knife or in a multiple saw pad. Draw guidelines on the veneered ends of the barn and assemble with glue. Brass screw eyes and a 12″ length of chain came from a hardware store.

To form the hex symbol for each end of barn, stars are knife-cut from mahogany. Quadrants forming circle around star are avodire.

Caul block roughly cut to fit end of barn distributes even clamping pressure while glue dries on veneered surface.

HANDCRAFTED VENEER JEWELRY

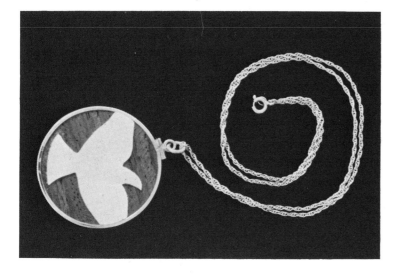

Your box of veneer leftovers contains pieces too small for most cutout designs, but it is a treasure chest of jewelry possibilities. Colorful odds and ends of veneer are ideal for designs that can be expressed in a small wood circle or square.

The prerequisite for handcrafted veneer jewelry is a suitable holder. It can be nickel or silver, and it must be reasonably large. Blank holders of this sort are called findings. Suitable findings include brooches, pins, pendants, key-chain fobs, and oversize cuff links and rings. Locate your findings before you lay out your designs. Local jewelry stores often stock circular bezels made to hold silver dollars. Smaller bezels to hold smaller coins are made but are harder to find.

Design ideas will tumble over each other when you decide to make veneer jewelry. Flowers, animals, birds, hobby motifs, sentimental themes, a monogram initial, and many other subjects are adaptable. The one important principle is simplicity. For a design to be recognized, it must be simple and bold. And for a design to be made of

veneer it must have a simple outline. Try out your design ideas by drawing them in silhouette to see how well they express your chosen theme and how practical they are to cut in veneer.

PENDANTS AND FOBS. A bezel for a silver dollar has a diameter of 1½″. The inside of the rim is grooved. When the knob fastening device is loosened, the bezel springs open. This feature permits a disc of veneer to be slipped into the groove, where it is held firmly once the bezel is tightened.

A one-piece or two-piece veneer cutout is cut separately and glued to the veneer disc. Most bezels are identical on both sides, which suggests using cutouts on both sides of the disc.

One thickness of veneer is not strong enough for a disc. At least three pieces must be glued together. You can either saw-cut or knife-cut a disc.

SAW-CUT DISC. Cut three pieces of veneer into 2¼″ squares. Following the core principle, Chapter 12, layer them together with glue, crisscrossing grain. You need three squares of $1/28''$ veneer or four squares of $1/40''$ veneer.

After it has dried, sandwich the assembled little panel in a saw pad and trace the outside of the bezel on the top pad. Cut the pad with your fret saw to produce a veneer disc.

KNIFE-CUT DISC. With your craft knife you can cut only one disc at a time. Trace and cut three individual circles ready for gluing into one disc.. Perfect the disc by sanding with an emery board as necessary to make a tight fit inside the bezel. Should the disc be loose, use glue to hold it in place; if visibly open at any place remove the disc and pad a small amount of matching sawdust and glue mix on the undercut perimeter.

FLOWER CUTOUT. The simple design of a wild sweetbriar rose was used for the jewelry cutout. With your knife you can cut one rose at a time and one flower center at a time. In a saw pad you can saw two roses and two centers at a time. Layer the pad with one piece of satinwood and one of pastel pink or any reddish veneer on hand. Cut around the petals first, and then go between two petals to cut the flower center. When you glue the centers to the disc mix them for contrast.

VENEER CREATES MODERN ART

Veneer enters the realm of abstract art in a project that can be both an artistic painting for hanging on a wall or a practical serving tray.

Essentially what abstract artists have done is to create paintings, the forms of which are nonsymmetrical, yet the proportion, color, and texture of the paintings give the impression of superb balance.

As a veneer craftsman you can copy the model developed here, or you can create your own designs and paint them with colorful veneer. This project started with the one-dollar purchase of an old picture frame. The proportion drawing was made to fit the frame. You can start the same way, with a secondhand frame, or you can develop your own painting on a hardboard panel of manageable size and then have the picture framed.

To make the picture, you need veneers, picture frame, and hardboard panel. Use a white crayon pencil to lay out accurate squares on the panel. The first veneer piece to glue down is the largest. Lay it accurately along the white guideline, letting it overhang the two edges of the panel. Use inlay border strips for dividers. Lay two dividers against the glued veneer. Add another veneer square after carefully fitting and trimming it to form a good joint against the border strip. Observe closely how each section of border is cut and laid. Trim off the overhang of veneer and border strip before laying the next piece. This assembly takes time, as the panel must go into clamps after each glue-down. Finish the frame with spray or brush before installing the picture.

To add the serving tray feature, cover the veneers with a pane of glass to fit the frame and use ½″ quarter-round molding underneath to form feet for the tray. After you have assembled the picture, glue long strips of molding under the long edges of the frame and short strips near the corners of the short edges. This leaves a space at the center of each short end to act as a handhold space for picking up the tray.

Lay largest veneer square first. Trim edges to avoid breaking. Next, lay adjoining border strips and second veneer square, edges overhanging.

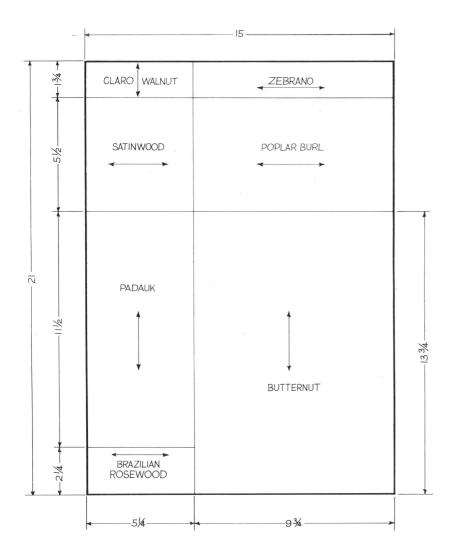

CLARO | WALNUT

ZEBRANO

SATINWOOD

POPLAR BURL

PADAUK

BUTTERNUT

BRAZILIAN
ROSEWOOD

15

3/4

5½

21

11½

2¼

13 ¾

5¼

9 ¾

VENEERED AND DECORATED BOXES

Ready-made, unfinished small boxes available at craft supply counters make ideal veneering projects. These close-grain basswood boxes provide an excellent gluing surface and they come in a tempting variety of sizes and shapes suitable for jewelry, keepsakes, musical units, playing cards, household coin bank, needles and thread, facial tissue boxes, and novelty purses.

Veneering techniques are nearly the same for all square and rectangular shapes, and these are the ones to select for your first veneered box project. If you apply beautiful veneer, no other decorative treatment is needed, but there are ways to add further decoration. The easiest way is with an overlay like the applied tiger on satiny, pale gold avodire. Another example is the eagle inlay on the walnut box. Special purpose boxes, too, are sold ready-made. An unfinished box with a slotted top and slip bottom, made to take a standard box of facial tissue, was veneered with makori (African cherry) and decorated with inlaid banding.

The box used as a demonstration project is decorated with a sunburst inlay. You can omit the inlay and still produce an attractive gift box.

SUNBURST BOX. Separate the lid from the box and handle the two sections as individual projects. Remove the hinges by carefully prying them up with the tip of a screwdriver. These are drive hinges, almost impossible to reinstall properly. Discard them and procure a pair of small brass screw hinges for installation after you have completed all veneering.

I selected mahogany pommelle, reddish brown with a curly figure, for the sunburst box. Veneer the lid first. Cut oversize strips for front, back, and two ends. Cut one piece for the top, also oversize to allow about $3/16''$ overhang at every edge.

Follow standard gluing techniques, applying only one panel at a time, allowing it to dry, and then trimming the overhang before gluing the next panel. The general rule for box veneering is to glue last what you see first. This practice—gluing back,

ends, front, and lid in that order—hides the most edge grain.

The last panel to lay down is the top. If you decide to inlay an inset, such as sunburst, refer to the simplified inlaying method in Chapter 12. Lay veneer on outside surfaces of the box section in the same way you handled the lid. If the box is intended for jewelry, line the inside with velvet. If for other purposes, paint inside surfaces before you veneer the outside.

Lay veneer on only one surface at a time. Wait for glue to dry before trimming overhang.

VENEERED PLANTER AND KNIFE KEEPER

Veneer can be laid on smooth metal surfaces, flat or rounded, with contact glue. The successful experiments shown here started with tin cans without rolled ridges. Most food cans have seams; you will have to locate cans without this bothersome feature.

Flexible veneer 1/64" thick bends easily around cans, even small soup-size cans. Most kinds of heavier veneer will split when you bend them, but you may be able to find a cooperative sheet in your assortment. Bear in mind that the grain must run vertically. For the larger can you need a sheet about 13" wide.

With a string, measure the circumference of the can to determine the width of veneer required. Measure inside the rolled lips to find the length. Apply veneer with contact glue. Brazilian rosewood was selected for the planter, walnut for the knife keeper.

TWELVE-PIECE TURTLE PUZZLE

A new pocket calculator was asked, "How many moves to solve the turtle puzzle?" It came up with 133 as the maximum number of moves required if you never make the same move twice.

Don't tell your friends what the object is that they are about to assemble. Only you are to know that it is a turtle. Actually it is two swimming turtles. It can be assembled as Turtle Northwest or Turtle Northeast as the photographs reveal.

If your friends surrender after a while, you can easily assemble the turtle puzzle in two or three minutes because you have inside information and can remember to start with three body squares of the same color, then build around those starters.

The trick that makes this turtle a little

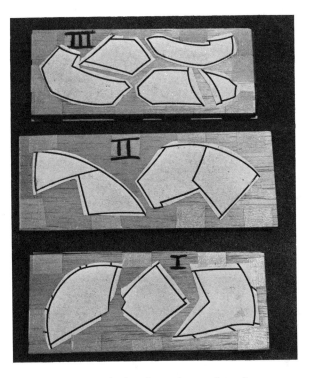

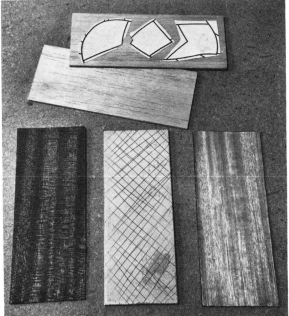

Turtle pattern is broken down for three saw pads. See schedule for contents of each pad.

Top pieces are top and bottom blinds of saw pad. Bottom left, sapele veneer. Center, venetian blind core scored for better glue bond. Right, primavera veneer. This assembly is based on the core principle for stabilizing small veneer cutouts.

brain-twister is the use of light wood, primavera, on one side of each body piece and dark wood, sapele, on the other side of each body piece. The head and four feet are light claro walnut on one side and dark claro walnut on the other side, a subtle difference which may be overlooked.

The person trying to solve the puzzle assumes that all light-colored pieces must somehow fit together, but they won't. It takes the right combination of light and dark.

The turtle puzzle is not difficult to make, but it demands close attention to working procedure. Because veneer is too brittle for handling as separate small pieces, you must turn to the practical core principle and the saw pad method.

You need three saw pads. You can substitute other light and dark woods, if you

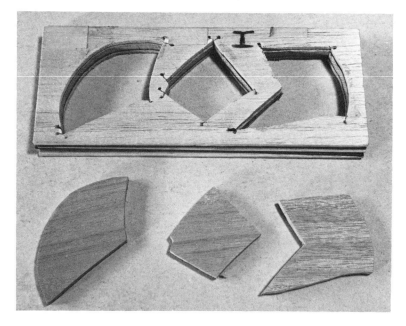

Pad I yields three pieces with primavera showing, sapele underneath.

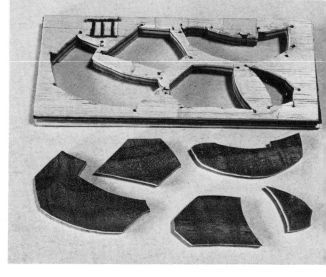

Pad III makes five pieces, dark walnut showing, light walnut underneath just to confuse the assembler further.

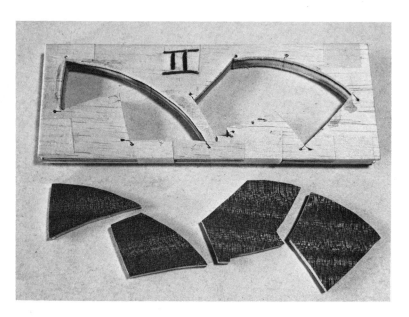

Pad II makes four pieces, sapele showing.

wish. Make your pattern breakup according to the illustration here. The core facing for each pad and placement in the pad must follow this schedule:

PAD I: 2⅜″ x 6″ top side primavera; bottom side sapele.

PAD II: 2⅜″ x 6½″ top side sapele; bottom side primavera.

PAD III: 2⅜″ x 6″ top side dark walnut; bottom side light walnut.

The turtle puzzle will show you that you can make other animal designs into simpler educational puzzles for children. Animals from "Africa Panorama," for instance, could be made easily by the core principle and saw pad method, but without the confusing mixture of different woods.

KING-SIZE CHESS SET

Thirty-two squares of colorful, highly figured veneer make a distinctively different chessboard. About twenty-five kinds of veneer are utilized. Some are laid with figure horizontally placed, some with vertical figure, some cut with figure on the diagonal. All veneers chosen for the project must be dark enough or distinctly colored enough to contrast with white maple.

In addition to looking different from the standard construction of alternating walnut and maple squares, this chessboard is easier to make than the standard style. All so-called dark squares are overlaid instead of inlaid. They are cut to identical size with your craft knife and are then glued to a ready-made maple plywood panel.

Once you get accustomed to the idea of overlaid squares, you will probably agree with those who have seen this demonstration model that overlaid squares present no problem whatever to chess players. Instead of sliding chessmen from square to square, a slight lift of the chessmen gets them where they are headed.

If you follow the easy course, you will start with a ready-made panel of ½″ plywood faced on one side with white maple. Try to obtain it cut to final size, or you will have to cut it by following the method detailed in Chapter 9. The king-size board is 24″ square. For it, make the veneer squares 2⅞″. The next smaller practical size is 18″ square. For that size, make the veneer squares 2⅛″. Either size you choose will leave a margin of ½″ at every edge.

For cutting identical squares, make a very accurate square template of hardboard. Don't settle for an imperfect edge on your template. It will be duplicated thirty-two times. Lay the template on veneer and cut a light guideline around it. Put the template aside and use your straightedge as a guide for completing the

cut. Observe all the rules for knife-cutting: lay a strip of clear tape underneath the cutting line and cut from edge to center. You need thirty-two perfect squares, but don't stop at thirty-two. Make a few spares for last-minute substitution in case an alternate color or figure would be an improvement. After using your template for marking all squares, now use it as a backup block for sanding the edges.

Lay flexible wood edging around border, allowing overhang. Overlap ends without glue.

Start assembly near the center after you have laid out light pencil guidelines and have trial-tested the squares you want to start with. Continue to assemble outward in every direction, making sure that all squares touch at corners.

After all the squares are glued down and allowed to dry, the completed assembly should have a ½″ margin. Before applying a border, in order to conceal the plywood edges of the panel, lay veneer edging around the edge of the panel. Then glue walnut or mahogany veneer edging on the

Cut loose ends to form miter at corners. Now glue down loose ends of border.

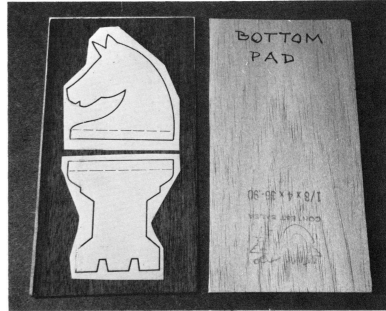

Chessmen, veneered on both sides, are built on core principle and are cut in open saw pad.

face to create a border. Lay it tightly against the veneer squares, letting the other edge overhang and the ends overlap.

Turn the panel over and trim off the overhang. Lay a straightedge across the overlapping edging at the corners and trim through two thicknesses to form a miter joint.

VENEER CHESSMEN. Your unique chessboard deserves chessmen of an innovative design. Chessmen have been made of everything from ivory to nuts and bolts, but never before of veneer. The chessmen illustrated are possible structurally because they are made according to the core principle in Chapter 12. The design for the figures is based on universal chess symbols. Wherever you see a chess game in print, you see chess symbols like the set you now can make.

Purpleheart veneer is used for the black figures, pale gold avodire for the white. Chessmen must be saw-cut. Glue purpleheart to both sides of ⅛″ poplar core. Make a bottom pad only. With rubber cement applied only around the perimeter, affix a pattern for two figures on one side of the veneer, following the open pad system. Glue avodire to other cores. You need the following figures in each color for a complete set:

1 king	2 bishops
1 queen	2 knights
2 rooks	8 pawns

For the king-size 24″ board, make chessmen 2⅝″ at the base, using the accompanying patterns. For the standard 18″ board, reduce the patterns to measure 2″ at the base.

The device which supports the chessmen is a pair of ¼″ thick solid wood blocks. Each chessman is glued between two blocks that provide a flat, stable base. To assure a flat base, improvise a clamping setup with a C-clamp pressing blocks against chessman

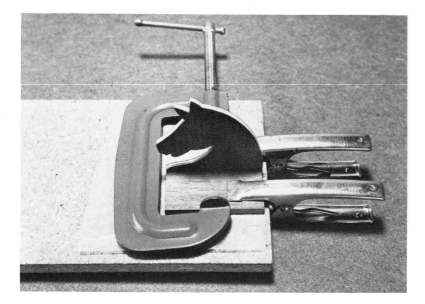

Follow two-way clamping arrangement to assure level base for knight and companion pieces.

and spring clamps pressing blocks against bottom caul board.

Blocks for the king-size set are 1¼" x 2⅝"; for the standard-size set, approximately ¹⁵/₁₆" x 2". Any attractive wood is suitable. Honduras rosewood was used for the model set.

SUGGESTED MATERIALS. For king-size chessboard: one maple plywood panel ½" x 24" x 24"; one box of 4" x 9" veneer sheets containing a large variety of veneers. Two rolls of veneer edging, walnut or mahogany. For chessmen: 4 sq. ft. avodire veneer; 4 sq. ft. purpleheart veneer. For chessmen bases: 2 sq. ft. ¼" Honduras rosewood. For chessmen saw pads: 4 sq. ft. balsa, ⅛" or ³/₃₂".

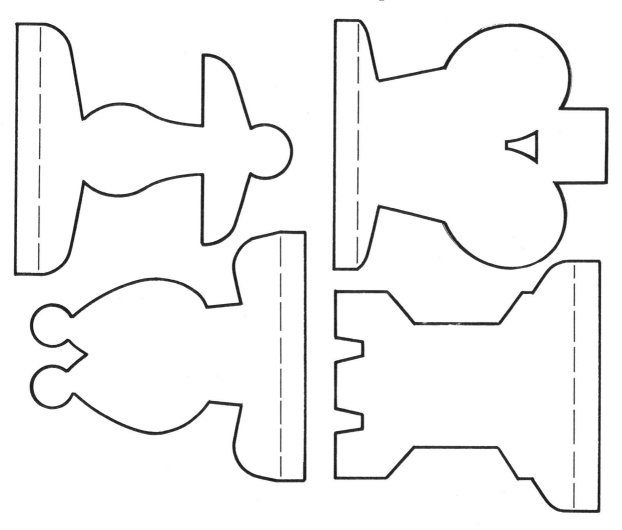

THE FABULOUS FLYING TRAPEZE MOBILE

The core principle detailed in Chapter 12 has many imaginative applications in veneer craft. The trapeze mobile could not be accomplished without the core principle.

Of course trapeze aerialists represent only one of the themes that lend themselves to three-dimensional interpretation for mobiles. When you think of alternate themes—birds, abstract 'modern shapes, the populated tree of life, and others—try your designs first as cardboard silhouettes

to make sure that their meaning comes through.

The idea for this simple, easily constructed mobile that flutters, spins, and travels up and down was carried out with hardware store items.

The central tent pole is a 3-foot length of threaded ⅜″ rod. The crossbars, or make-believe tightropes, are ⅛″ threaded rod. The longest one, at the top, is 3 feet long. The other two were cut a couple of inches shorter, as dictated by the location

of figures, swings, and drop rope. Nuts to fit the upright rod were grooved with a file to let in the crossbars, and the crossbars were soldered to the nuts. In addition, you need two nuts and two washers to secure the upright rod to the wood base.

Any 9″ wood block can serve as a base. The fancy one in the model was made of three pieces of ½″ zebrano, cherry, and East Indian rosewood. Wood squares are scalloped, bored for the rod, and the bottom one counterbored underneath for washer and nut.

To create the volute, or spiral carving, turn the middle block ½″ to the left, and turn the top block another ½″. Glue the blocks in this voluted position. With a wood rasp, lots of sandpaper, and plenty of work, carve the jagged scalloped volutes into a smoothly flowing spiral curve.

For each aerialist, face ⅛″ core on both sides with pastel pink veneer or with your own choice. Saw-cut the figures to shape in open saw pads. Walnut veneer is used for the chimpanzee. For full-size pattern of it, see "Africa Panorama."

Suspend the swinging figures on pink thread. No holes are necessary. Use a double loop; that is, drop two open strands from crossbar to figure. By experiment you will discover how the double loop reduces spinning to a desirable minimum.

Spot-glue the foot of the lady on the platform where she can acknowledge cheers from the crowd after a breathtaking performance. Ropes for two swings and drop rope are dressmaker's cord sprayed gold. If the ultimate in showmanship appeals to you, focus a spotlight bulb on your fanciful circus act.

Lady on drop rope holds it in position for flying aerialist far below.

Blocks are glued together in offset formation to start the volute. Carved effect of volute is produced with rasp. A square base would hold the mobile just as well.

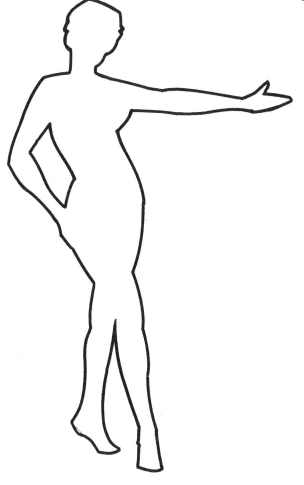

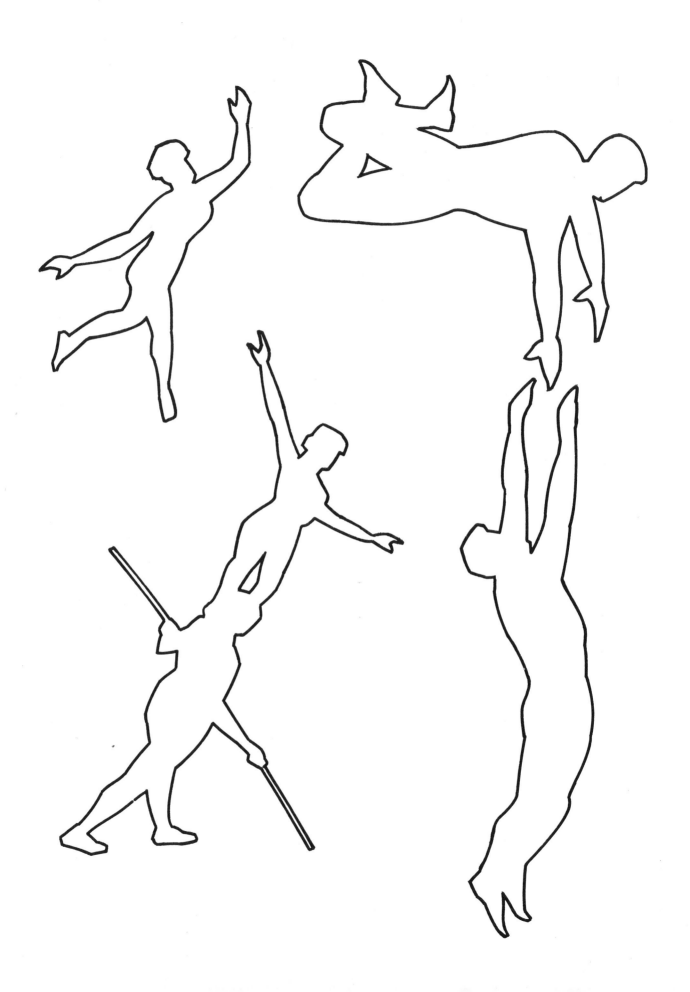

CHAPTER 15

Introduction to Marquetry— Simplified Procedure

The terms "inlay" and "marquetry" are often used interchangeably. Most often a marquetry picture is mistakenly called an inlay picture. Here the terms will be used for different types of work.

Inlay refers to the process by which any of a variety of thin materials is inset into a recessed solid surface. The center sunburst design, bought ready-made, was inlaid into the veneered box top.

The picture of "Bighorn II" (Figure 85) on the rocky cliff is marquetry. The cutout parts of veneer were assembled into a one-piece veneer face, and the face was glued to a mounting panel.

There are several ways to make a marquetry picture. The simple method demonstrated here could have been accomplished entirely with a craft knife. However, because I happen to find the saw a more accurate method of cutting joints, I used the fret saw to cut the three members for the Bighorn panel. For practical reasons, the opening in the face for the separate animal cutout was cut with a knife.

Briefly, the system is this: first you cut and assemble only the background veneer. You cut Bighorn separately and inset the

Figure 85. "Bighorn II" is a marquetry picture. The animal is inset into a three-piece veneer background to form a one-piece level assembly for mounting on a panel. The demonstrated method is easy for beginners. (See p. 26 for full-size pattern.)

147

cutout into the background veneer assembly; and then you glue the entire veneer face to the panel. This system wastes veneer somewhat because it starts with 8½" x 11" sheets, but some of the leftover pieces can be salvaged for smaller projects.

MATERIALS

mounting panel—flakeboard ⅜" x 8" x 10½"
backing—mahogany veneer 8½" x 11"
edging—mahogany edging tape 30"
sky—avodire veneer 6" x 8½"
cliff—chinawood veneer 8½" x 11"
mountain/valley—maple burl veneer
    8½" x 11"
Bighorn—butt walnut veneer 4" x 6"
top pad and patches—poplar veneer
    12" x 24"
bottom pad—balsa 12" x 12"
glue and gummed paper tape

Begin this project by preparing a mounting panel, veneering the back and edges as demonstrated earlier.

For the face, select and cut three sheets of contrasting veneer that depict what they represent. The illustrated model used an effective combination, but there are many other choices just as appealing.

The chinawood sheet was patched in the waste areas of the corners where the sheet was damaged. Only a small sheet of avodire was on hand, and it was extended with a patch of poplar waste. Patching is good practice because full-size sheets make the pad level and more stable. The bottom saw pad was made of two pieces of balsa taped together. Pad components are shown in Figure 86.

Sheets of veneer are oversize, allowing overhang at all edges of the mounting panel. Each veneer sheet and the top blind of the saw pad are numbered in sequence.

Figure 86. Components of saw pad to make the interlocking marquetry background veneer. Veneers in numbered order are: avodire, maple burl, chinawood. At lower right, cutting outlines have been traced on top blind of saw pad.

Number 1, avodire, has to produce the sky, number 1 area outlined on the saw pad.

Number 2, maple burl, represents a distant mountain and approaching valley. This sheet produces the number 2 area outlined on saw pad. The sheet of burl you see was cut from a large, irregular piece of veneer, and the area was narrowed down by the use of the viewer suggested in Chapter 6. Notice the results of this careful selection by referring to the finished marquetry picture: the maple burl has become a rock-layered mountain sloping toward the valley.

Number 3, chinawood, was cut on the diagonal to provide a steep, layered, rocky cliff for Bighorn's lookout. Diagonal cutting didn't produce a perfect piece because the sheet on hand had several splits. This is a brittle veneer. Corners had to be taped to make full-size sheets of veneer for the pad, but the taped splits do not show in the finished picture.

ASSEMBLING THE BACKGROUND SAW PAD.

On tracing paper, draw your own design for the background: one jagged line to mark off the cliff, another for the division between sky and mountain. Trace this pattern onto the top saw pad. Sandwich the three veneer sheets between top and bottom pads. You can spot-glue waste areas of the bottom veneer to the bottom saw pad. This helps to stabilize the large pad, but gluing means that you forego usable chinawood leftovers. Tape the pad tightly around all edges.

CUTTING THE PAD.

Sawing requires a deep-throat fret saw (Figure 87) to swing around the corners of the pad to make neatly interlocking pieces for the background. Cut the saw pad and veneers into three sections. Bind the cut edges with tape until you are ready to take each section apart.

ASSEMBLING BACKGROUND VENEERS.

Open each pad section and pull out the three useful pieces. Fit them together, face side up, and bind together at the joints, using precut 1″ pieces of gummed paper tape. You sponge and peel off tape later.

CUTTING AND INSETTING BIGHORN.

There are two ways to cut Bighorn. You can trace the outline directly onto a sheet

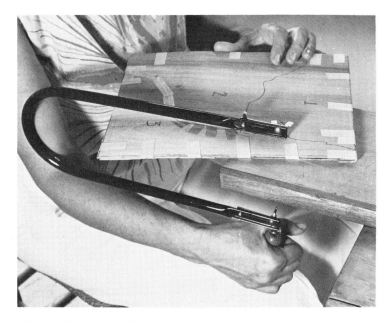

Figure 87. Use a deep-throat fret saw that can swing around corners of pad. Cut off area number 3 first, working from bottom edge to top. This order makes the next cut easy.

of veneer and cut the animal with your craft knife. Or, as I did here, you can trace the outline of Bighorn onto the top member of a saw pad containing a square of butt walnut veneer and saw around the outline, using a fret saw. Remove your cutout from the pad and touch up any rough edges with sandpaper.

Cut the opening for Bighorn in the assembled veneer face, using the animal cutout as a template. Turn the veneer face over, face down. Turn Bighorn over, face down. Fix the position with three short lengths of paper tape. Trace around the animal with your craft knife or with a very sharp pencil. Move the tape, one piece at a time, and complete the tracing. Cut the prescribed opening for Bighorn (Figure 88). When cutting, try to keep inside the line to make the opening a tight fit. You can easily sand the opening or the cutout to make a perfect fit.

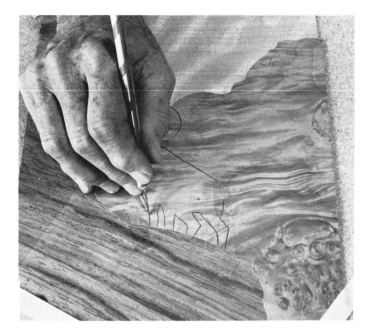

Figure 88. Use craft knife to cut Bighorn outline completely through veneer assembly. Cut somewhat inside the traced outline to assure tight fit. Bighorn cut from opening becomes waste.

Figure 89. Inset walnut Bighorn into opening cut in veneer assembly. Secure with tape on the face side.

Inset Bighorn. Turn the veneer assembly right side up. Fit the walnut animal cutout in place and fix its position with paper tape on the front face (Figure 89).

Fill the joints. Scrape sawdust from a scrap of maple burl. Use it with white glue to fill all joints from the back (Figure 90). Hold the veneer assembly up to the light occasionally to locate places that need more filling.

Glue the assembled veneer face to your previously prepared background panel (Figure 91). Because it is important to place your veneer assembly accurately on the panel, draw guidelines on veneer, lay panel on veneer, and trace around it. Next, spread glue on veneer and lay panel on guidelines. The alternate method of laying a dry veneer face blind on a glue-fresh panel cannot be done so accurately.

Set in clamps for overnight. Clamps are preferable to weights for a large veneer face composed of several veneers which may vary slightly in thickness.

Figure 90. This is the back of the assembly. Scrape a filler mix of sawdust and glue into joints. This is the standard way marquetry pictures are touched up.

Trim overhanging edges, moisten and remove gummed tape from the face, and fill joints from the front if necessary. Finishing is optional.

MARQUETRY LESSON NUMBER TWO.

The simplified marquetry technique demonstrated for Bighorn can be carried somewhat further. Instead of Bighorn a more complex design is required. Let us use "The Vanishing American" as our subject.

Make a three-piece background veneer face of the Western plains, composed of sky, distant hills, and broad approaching plain. Working on the underside of this veneer assembly, cut an opening in the background and inset a veneer cutout of the Indian's horse just as you inset Bighorn. Ignore the Indian in this step. Inset a complete horse without a rider. Tape it in position. Next, make a separate cutout of the Indian rider. Using it as a template,

Figure 91. Prepared mounting panel, veneered on back, is now laid on glue-fresh back of veneer assembly. Guidelines drawn on veneer assure accurate placement. It is better practice to spread glue on panel when you have the option, but no difficulties arose from alternate procedure followed here.

and again working on the underside of the veneer assembly, trace the Indian cutout in position on the horse. Now cut around the traced outline to make an opening for the rider. You will be cutting through part of the horse and part of the background and in some places through tape. With a little extra care you can cut this opening successfully because the horse remains taped to the background. Place temporary snips of clear tape behind your knife as you cut. When you have finished cutting, remove tape to get the waste piece out of the opening. Turn the assembly over. Fit and tape the rider into position on the horse. You now have a marquetry veneer face with Indian and rider in position. The assembly is ready for gluing to a mounting panel of hardboard.

You probably have already surmised that the insetting system of marquetry could be carried still further. You could have inset a few clumps of sagebrush, foreground rock formation, or other decoration. Eventually this system reaches its limit. For one thing, the pileup of gummed tape becomes too much to deal with. It is, however, an ideal introductory method for the beginner, as it promises greater success than other marquetry methods.

In its advanced stages, at the hands of practiced marquetarians, marquetry is an exacting craft and a highly rewarding one. The techniques learned from veneer craft projects in this book prepare you for marquetry. In fact, many of the operations performed are identical to what you do when creating marquetry pictures.

There is now an active Marquetry Society of America whose members set up gallery shows of their work, exchange work experiences, and pass along improved techniques which they have discovered or simplified in the course of picture-making.

APPENDIX

Suppliers

1. Art supply stores
2. Brookstone Company
   Peterborough, N.H. 03458
3. Albert Constantine and Son, Inc.
   2050 Eastchester Road
   Bronx, N.Y. 10461
4. Craftsman Wood Service Co.
   2729 South Mary Street
   Chicago, Ill. 60608
5. Craft supply stores

6. Jewelry stores
7. Lumberyards and
   building supply dealers
8. Metal City Findings Corp.
   450 West 31st Street
   New York, N.Y. 10001
9. Woodcraft Supply Corp.
   313 Montvale Avenue
   Woburn, Mass. 01801

Sources of Supply

MATERIALS

boxes, unfinished 3, 5
fret-saw blades 2, 3, 4
fret saws 3, 4, 9
glue 3, 4, 5, 9
graph paper 1
grid sheets, transparent 1
insets 3, 4
jewelry findings 6, 8
knives 1, 3, 4, 5

molding, framing 1, 3, 7
mounting panels 3, 4, 7
patterns 1, 3, 5
saw table 3
veneers 3, 4
veneer saws 3, 4, 9
wood finish 3, 4
woodworking tools 2, 3, 4, 9

Index

Advanced techniques, 71–78
  general procedure for, 74–75
Assembled veneer faces, 12
Avodire, 10

Basic workshop, tools for, 6–7
Bird's-eye maple, 10
Butternut, 10

Cardboard templates, 35
Cardboard viewer, 31–32
Cauls, 16–17, 56
Chinawood, 10–11
Chisel blade for cutting, 38
Clamping cutouts, 64
Clamps, 16, 19
Cleaning and finishing, 65–70
  applying the finish, 68–69
  brushing, 67
  edges, 66–67
  filling joints, 65–66
  framing the picture, 69–70
  nameplates, 70
  sanding assembled cutouts, 67
  touch up, 67–68
Complete-picture pad, 45
Core principle, 77
Cutouts, applying, 59–64
  clamping, 64
  gluing, 61–62
  guidelines for, 61
  laying out panoramic displays, 61
  sanding, 59–61
  trial assembly, 59
  weighting, 62–64
Cutting techniques, 34–50
  knife, 34–39
  saw, 40–50

Designs and patterns, 21–24
  enlarging or reducing, 23
  frog pattern (enlarged), 23–24
  how to reverse, 24
  symmetrical shapes, 24
Drills, 19
Dyed veneers, 11–12

Edging, flexible veneer for, 12
Enlarging a design, 23
Equipment. *See* Tools and equipment

Filling joints, 65–66
Flakeboard, 52–53
Frames, picture, 69–70
French curve, 35
Fret saws, 17–18, 40

Glue bubbles, 67
Glues, 14–15
Gluing
  aids for, 15
  cutouts, 61
  for mounting panels, 55
Guidelines (pencil), 61
Gumwood, 11

Inlaying, 72–74

Jig saws, types of, 19–20
Joining two sheets, 53

Knife blades, 13
Knife-cut disc, 131
Knife-cutting techniques, 34–39
  cardboard templates, 35
  chisel blade, 38
  for intricate parts, 36–38
  razor blade, 38
  safety precautions, 38–39
  for small parts, 36
  specialty templates, 35
  taping the back, 34–35
  template method, 54–55
  tracing the pattern, 34
  using knife and straightedge, 35–36
  veneer characteristics and, 34
  veneer templates, 35
Knives, 13

Mahogany, 11
Marquetry, 147–51

assembling the background saw pad, 149
background veneers, 149
cutting and insetting, 149–51
materials, 148–49
Mitering borders, 71–72
Mixed saw pad system, 41–42
Mounting panels for cutouts, 51–58
  cauls, 56
  clamping, 55
  cutting plywood, 51
  edging, 57–58
  gluing techniques, 55
  joining two sheets, 53
  knife-cutting method, 54–55
  multi-piece background techniques, 53–54
  preparing veneer, 53
  pre-sanding parts, 57
  ready-made, 51
  sanding the edges, 57
  trimming, 56–57
Multiple saw pad system, 41

Nameplates, 70

Oak, 11
Open pad method, 45
Overlay, meaning of, 4

Panoramic displays, laying out, 61
Patch pad system, 42–45
Picture gallery, 125–29
  arranging, 125
  easy display method, 125
  shadow box display, 125–27
Plywood panels, cutting, 51–52
Power jig saws, 19–20
Pre-sanding veneer parts, 57
Primavera, 10
Problems, correcting, 79–82
Projects, 83–124
  "Africa Panorama," 2, 4, 11, 61, 69, 120–24, 144
  barn purse box, 128–29
  "Bighorn I," 5, 26, 67

Projects (continued)
    "Bighorn II," 10, 88, 147–51
    "Birds in Flight," 4, 25, 40–41, 88–89
    boxes, 133–35
    "Chariot Horse Frieze," 106–9
    chess set, 139–43
    "Discovery of America," 29, 38, 52, 103–4
    "Fabulous Flying Trapeze Mobile," 143–46
    "First Swimming Lesson," 24, 109–11
    "Flying Angel," 4, 41
    jewelry, 130–31
    key finder, 128
    knife keeper, 135–36
    "Last Supper, The," 68, 92–93
    "Lion's Pride," 11, 41, 112–13
    "Madonna," 71, 98–99
    "Mexico," 10, 11, 44, 52, 105–6
    "Midnight Ride of Paul Revere," 99–101
    planter, 135–36
    "Playful Panda," 38, 96–97
    "Prehistoric America," 2, 11, 69, 116–20
    "Reclining Lion," 26–27
    "Sports Gallery," 4, 11, 62, 83–88
    toast tongs, 127–28
    tray, 130–33
    "Tree of Life," 21, 22
    "Twelve-Piece Turtle Puzzle," 136–39
    "Two Fishermen," 101–3
    "Undersea World," 2, 61, 93–94
    "Vanishing American, The," 151
    "White Roses," 89–91
    "Wild Horses of Wyoming," 2, 11, 114–15

Razor-cutting techniques, 38
Ready-made mounting panels, 51
Reducing a design, 23
Reinforcing the pad, 46–48
Reverse pattern, 24
Rubber cement, 15

Sabre saw, 19
Sanding cutouts, 59–61, 67
Sanding panel edges, 57

Sandpaper, 19
Saw blades, 18
Saw-cut disc, 130–31
Saw-cutting techniques, 40–50
Saw pad construction, 45–46
Saw pads
    complete-picture pad, 45
    mixed pad, 41–42
    multiple pads, 41
    for one-piece designs, 40–41
    open pad method, 45
    opening saw pads, 50
    patch pad, 42–45
    reinforcement, 46–48
    work-feed, 49–50
Saw table, 49
    and clamp, 19
Saws
    blades, 18
    fret, 17–18
    power jig saw, 19–20
    scroll, 20
    veneer, 17
Selecting cutouts, 29–33
    avoiding monotony in, 30–31
    cardboard viewer and, 31–32
    contrast and background, 29–30
    cutting and cross-cutting, 32–33
Shadow box display, 125–27
Sharpening stone, 13
Specialty templates, 35
Spring clamps, 16
Straightedge, 14
Styrofoam, 13
Sycamore, 11
Symmetrical design, how to draw, 24

Tamo ash, 11
Tape, kinds of, 19
"Telegraphing," 16–17
Tool box, 19
Tools and equipment, 13–20
    for basic workshop, 6–7
    cauls, 16–17
    clamps, 16
    drills, 19
    glue and accessories, 14–15
    knives and blades, 13
    miscellaneous, 19
    power jig saw, 19–20

    sandpaper, 19
    saw table and clamp, 19
    saws and saw blades, 17–18, 19–20
    sharpening stone, 13
    straightedge, 14
    tool box, 19
    weights, 15
    wood for saw pads, 18
    workboard (caul board), 13–14
    workboxes, 19
    for workshop number 2, 7–8
Trimming, 56–57

Veneer craft
    advanced techniques, 71–78
    cutouts, 39–70
    designs and patterns, 21–24
    getting started, 4–8
    history of, 1–2
    marquetry, 147–51
    meaning of, 2, 4
    selling, 2–3
    tools and equipment, 13–20
    work patterns, 25–28
    See also Projects
Veneer saw, 17
Veneer templates, 35
Veneers
    dyed wood, 11–12
    for edging, 12
    kinds of, 9–12
    lengths and widths, 9–10
    meaning of, 4
    ready-to-use faces, 12
    selecting for cutouts, 29–33
    thicknesses, 11
    See also names of woods

Walnut, 11
Warp, correcting, 79–80
Weighting, 62–64
Weights, 15
Woods for saw pads, 18
Work patterns, preparing, 25–28
Workboard (caul board), 13–14
Workboxes, 19

X-acto knife, 13

Zebrano, 11